Using Microsoft Word to Write Research Papers in APA Style

Larry A. Pace, Ph.D.

ISBN 978-0-9799775-5-8
Published by TwoPaces.com
102 San Mateo Dr.
Anderson, SC 29625

Camera-ready text produced by the author. All web addresses shown in this book were correct at the time of printing. Visit TwoPaces.com at http://www.twopaces.com

About the Author

Dr. Larry Pace is an award-winning professor of psychology, statistics, research methods, mathematics, sociology, and management. He has taught at the college level for more than 35 years. He has been a professor, a department chair, a program coordinator for a master's degree program, an MBA program director, and a college dean. In addition to his continuing academic career, Dr. Pace worked as an internal and external business consultant, facilitator, trainer, researcher, manager for a Fortune 100 company, and business owner. He has consulted with organizations including Xerox Corporation, the U.S. Navy, International Paper, AT&T, Lucent Technologies, Compaq Computers, Tandem Computers, and UOP.

"Dr. Larry," as his students call him, earned the Ph.D. from the University of Georgia, majoring in psychometrics (applied statistics) and industrial psychology. He has taught statistics from the freshman level to the doctoral level, including mathematical statistics, business statistics, educational statistics, and behavioral statistics. He also teaches a variety of research methods courses at the undergraduate and graduate levels, as well as courses in psychology, mathematics, management, sociology, and leadership. He has published a wide variety of articles, reviews, and books, in addition to hundreds of online reviews and tutorials.

He has taught online and classroom-based courses and seminars at a number of colleges and universities including Walden University, Keiser University, Argosy University, Ashford University, University of the Rockies, Tri-County Technical College, Anderson University (where he was the chair of the behavioral sciences department), Clemson University, Capella University, Austin Peay State University, Louisiana Tech University (where he was the coordinator for the master's program in industrial psychology), Louisiana State University in Shreveport (where he was the acting dean of the business college for a year and the MBA program director before that), the University of Tennessee, Rochester Institute of Technology, Monroe Community College, Cornell University, Rensselaer Polytechnic Institute, and the University of Georgia. In 1997, he was an invited lecturer in the College of Business at the University of Jyväskylä in Finland. He won the Servant Leadership award from Anderson University, and was recognized by LSU-Shreveport for his research and teaching contributions. Dr. Pace won the Psi Chi professor of the quarter award from Louisiana Tech University.

His current research involves statistics education, the study of human error in data entry, the use of technology in education, and an ongoing exploration of students' and faculty members' attitudes toward plagiarism and other forms of academic dishonesty. He has presented dozens of papers, poster sessions, and invited addresses at the meetings of the American Psychological Association, the Association for Psychological Science, the National Institute on the Teaching of Psychology, and other organizations.

Dr. Pace lives in Anderson, SC. He is married to Shirley Pace. The Paces have four grown children and two grandsons. They are active community volunteers with Meals on Wheels and the Keep America Beautiful campaign. They are also pet lovers and rescuers with (currently) six cats and one dog.

Among many hobbies and interests, Dr. Pace enjoys a wide variety of cuisines, reading and writing about statistics, writing poems, making music (he plays several musical instruments), learning Spanish, reading about science and technology, doing number puzzles and word games, cooking on the grill, tending a small vegetable garden, woodcarving, and hosting gatherings for friends and family. His most unusual hobby is developing spreadsheet models for various statistical procedures. He shares these worksheets freely with his colleagues and students.

Preface and Acknowledgments

Many books present the use of American Psychological Association (APA) style for research papers, but such books rarely provide specific details about using a word processing program like Microsoft Word to achieve the more complicated aspects of APA formatting. Such books also typically help minimally, if at all, to improve students' writing. There are many excellent style manuals, and every good writer should have one or more of these at hand, along with the appropriate formatting instructions for the particular standard being followed. This book is a how-to survival manual for students, researchers, and faculty members who need to learn and use APA style and who would like to use some of the tools provided by Microsoft Word. If you are hoping to find out how to use Microsoft Word 2007, 2010, or 2011 more effectively for writing and formatting your research papers, you have come to the right place!

First as a student, and later as a researcher and professor, I had to learn and apply the formatting standards of APA. I am now a college professor, and I have been teaching at the college level for more than 35 years. Over the course of those many years, I have graded many hundreds (more likely thousands, to be truthful) of student papers. The APA formatting standards have changed over the years as electronic publishing has become more prevalent and has now become the norm rather than the exception.

Students and faculty members in any discipline can benefit from using the built-in features of Microsoft Word to help them with their research papers, class projects, theses, and dissertations. Many colleges and universities require student papers to be produced in Microsoft Word, and students often must use a standardized format such as that described in the publication manual of APA (2010). Although I certainly do not intend for this book to replace the APA manual, I address many of the issues students face when trying to format their papers in APA style, and I explain and illustrate ways in which the built-in features of Word can be of great assistance in achieving correct APA style. Because this is a book rather than an APA-style research paper, I do not adhere to APA style here, but I do address and illustrate how to use APA style in your research papers.

If you do not have one of the newest versions of Word, which are Word 2010 for Windows and Word 2011 for Mac as I write this, there are many good reasons to upgrade. Many new computers come with Word already installed, and the student version of Word is relatively inexpensive. Many college and university bookstores provide low-priced copies of Microsoft Office for students. If you have any version later than Word 2003, this manual will be helpful to you, but if you have Word 2010 or 2011, it will be even more helpful. Much of what I write here also applies to Word 2011 for Macs. If you have a Mac, your screens will look different from the ones in this book, which were taken as screen shots from Word 2010 for Windows, but Word 2011 for Mac has all the features of Word 2010!

I intentionally take an informal approach in this book, explaining things to you as we go along. Imagine you and I are sitting together in front of your computer and I am helping you figure out how to format your paper. Although the APA manual says to avoid the "editorial we," I use we intentionally in this book not to refer to myself, but to you, the reader, and myself, the author, as we converse.

Screen shots from Word 2010 show you exactly what to do, and I explain in plain English how to do it. You will learn tips and tricks for making Word work more efficiently, as well as how to get all (or at least most) the formatting points on your papers. My advice is to use this as a workbook, make notes, and try to duplicate the screen shots you see in the book.

The topics covered in this book developed from my corrections to student papers, as well as my own errors in formatting pointed out by my colleagues and editors. I have analyzed the common mistakes students (and many faculty members) make, and I address them in detail in this book, showing you how to avoid or correct them if you are making any of these mistakes yourself. In the process of providing feedback to students, I realized most students (and many faculty members, too) simply do not know how to use their computers as well as they should. To help my own students, I wrote extensive tutorials, but I found myself saying the same thing repeatedly. I finally concluded that the tutorials needed to be expanded into a book so students would have a survival manual to help them with their research papers, and faculty members would have a guidebook to help them evaluate the format of student papers.

Common trouble spots include page headers, page breaks, headings, in-text citations, and reference lists. Although the APA manual covers all these items, it does not tell readers how to accomplish the correct format using the features of Word or any other word processing program.

Although this is not a writing manual, I address some of the common writing mistakes students make in their papers, and I tell you how to fix or avoid those as well. The APA manual addresses some, but not all, of these issues.

No book is ever the work of a single individual, even when there is a single identified author. Although I write, edit, and illustrate many of my own books, including this one, I would not publish such an important book as this one without having the book externally reviewed. I am very grateful to my good friend and colleague Dr. Kathleen Andrews for her reviews and invaluable advice on this and several others of my other books. If you think I am an "APA formatting guru," you should meet Kate! I am privileged to have the advice and external review of my good friend and colleague Dr. Lê Xuân Hy of Seattle University. Dr. Hy and his students have classroom tested several of my books, and he has served on the review panel for this and several others of my texts. Dr. Sue Adragna of Keiser University, another APA-formatting whiz, carefully reviewed Chapter 4, making valuable comments and corrections. Some of my students also graciously consented to read and use this book in its draft versions. They provided helpful feedback on its readability, usefulness, and contents. Of course, I must bear the responsibility for any remaining mistakes, but all these individuals have been very helpful in catching errors and making the book more useful.

I would like to thank my wife Shirley Pace for her great sense of humor, her constant encouragement, for tolerating me while I read her some of the most egregious writing errors in student papers, and putting up with my obsessions with teaching, statistics, and APA style. Although I like reading and writing books and articles about statistics, Shirley prefers Stephen King novels. I once told a student that my wife and I often sit on the sofa with our respective reading choices, and the student said, "Well, Dr. Pace, they're the same, really–both scary!"

Brief Contents

Table of Contents

Chapter 1—Working With Word

As the capabilities of Microsoft Word grew over the years, versions of Word from 1997 to 2003 suffered from what my engineering friends call "*creeping elegance.*" Menus had submenus, which sometimes had additional submenus. Finding a particular option became increasingly difficult as the features of the program increased.

Comparing Word 2010 to Previous Versions

Here is the Microsoft Word 2003 interface (Figure 1). Observe how many toolbars, menus, and submenus there are. The interface is cluttered and confusing.

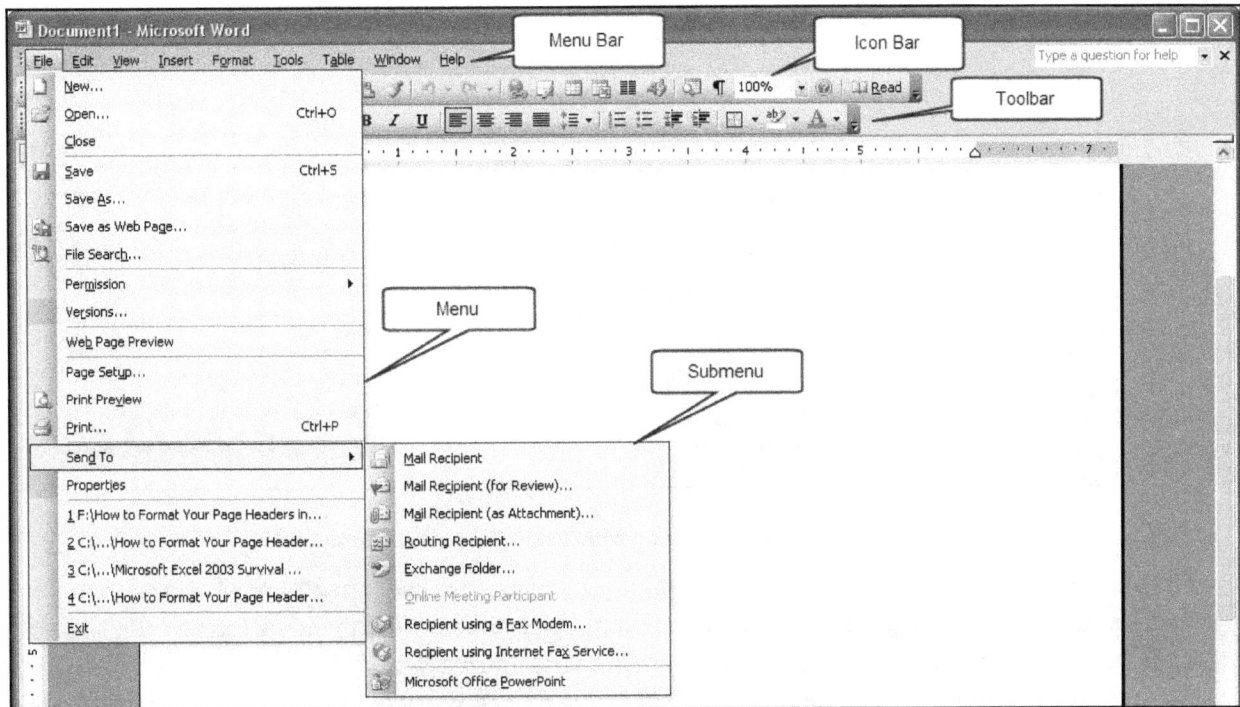

Figure 1. The Word 2003 interface

With Office 2007, Microsoft introduced the *ribbon*, a streamlined "super menu" that provides access to everything you can do with Word, either behind the scenes or in the current document. Office 2007 applications also have a round Office button, which makes the different programs more consistent. Below (Figure 2) is the Microsoft Word 2007 interface. Although it takes some getting used to, it is not quite as cluttered as the interface of Word 2003.

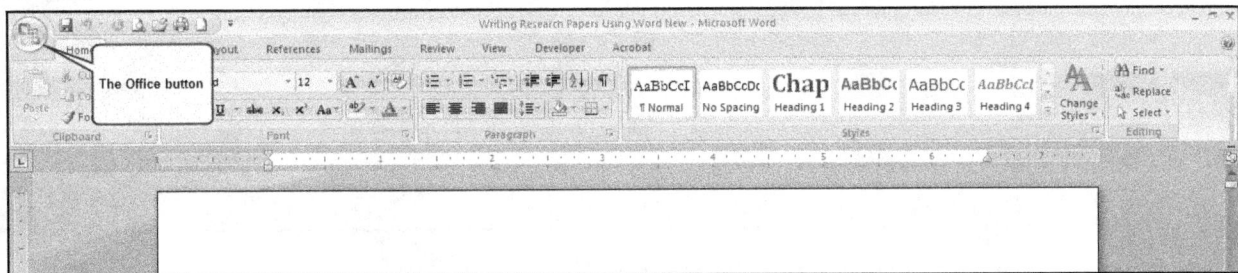

Figure 2. Microsoft Word 2007

The Microsoft Word 2010 Interface: Tabs, Ribbons, and Groups

With Office 2010, Microsoft kept the tab-and-ribbon layout of Office 2007, but replaced the Office button with a File tab to the left of the Home tab. Figure 3 shows the major features of the Microsoft Word 2010 interface. The Word 2007 interface is very similar, as you can see above (Figure 2). Depending on your own configuration, and which add-ins and toolbar items you might have activated, your interface may not have all the tabs or icons mine does. Your Quick Access Toolbar will not look like mine either, because I have customized mine, as we will discuss later. The ribbon expands and contracts based on the screen resolution, and the detail increases as the screen size increases.

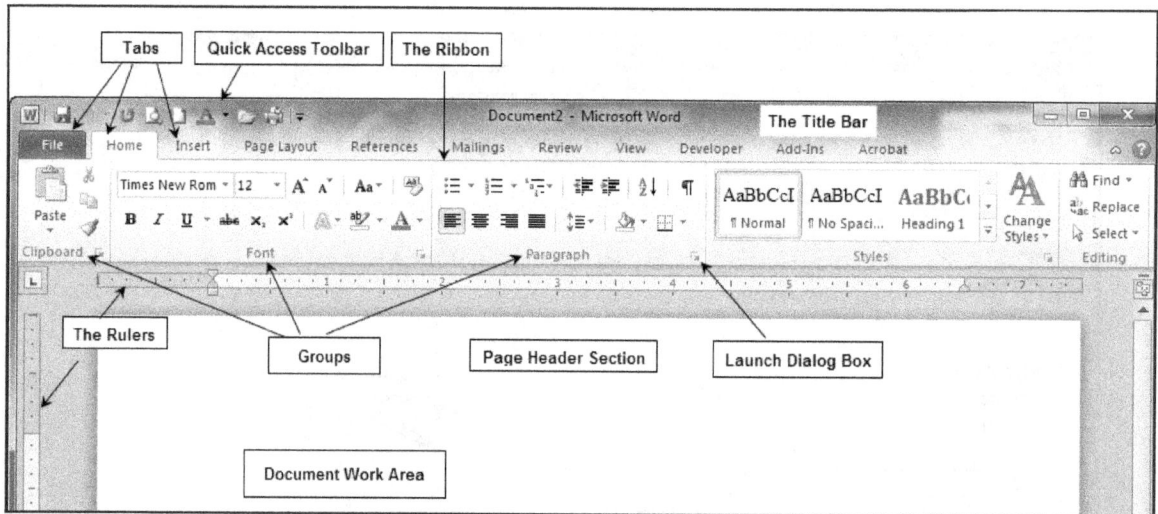

Figure 3. The Microsoft Word 2010 interface

Examine Word's tab-and-ribbon hierarchy. Notice on the ribbon there are groups of related commands and features, and many of the groups have additional options available when you click on a little box with an arrow at the bottom right corner of the group. Clicking there will launch a new dialog box for that particular group. If you hold the mouse pointer over a button or command, this causes Word to pop up a box with a description of the result of clicking on that button or command. To illustrate, hover over the icon that launches the Paragraph dialog box. Notice the result as follows (Figure 4).

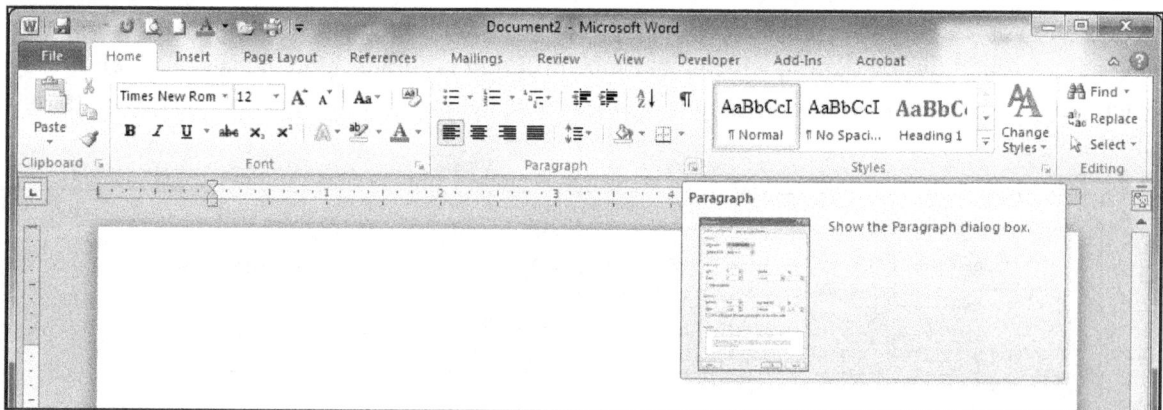

Figure 4. Holding the mouse pointer over the icon shows a preview of the dialog box

Below is the Paragraph dialog box. You can change the spacing and indentation here. APA style requires documents to be double spaced throughout with no extra spacing between paragraphs (see Figure 5).

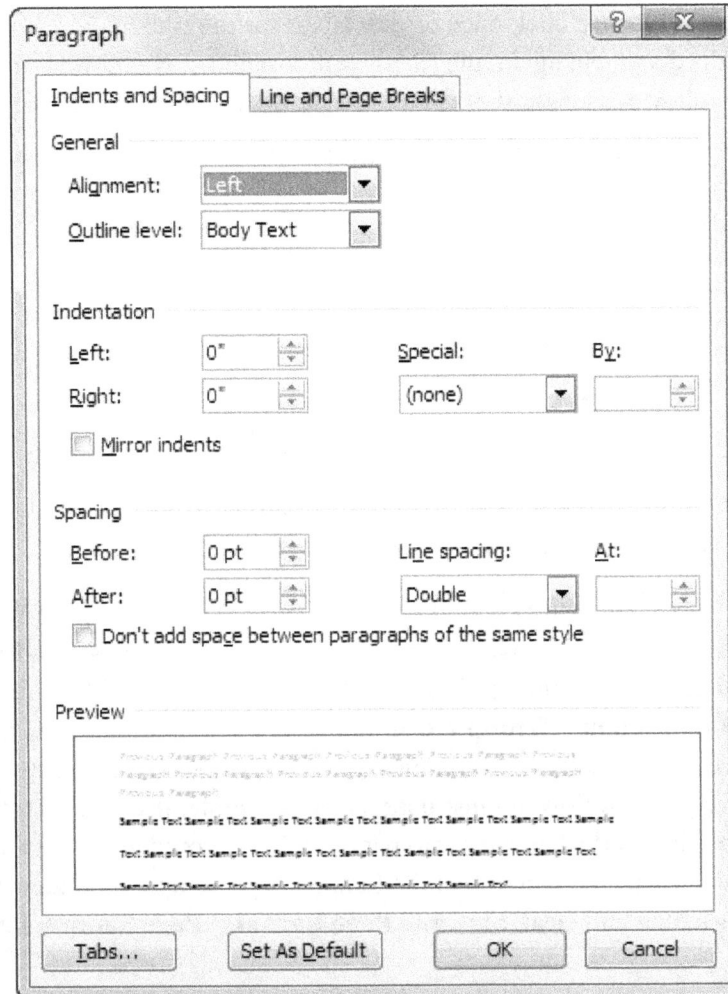

Figure 5. The Paragraph dialog box

You can also change the spacing via the Paragraph group in the Home ribbon (see Figure 6).

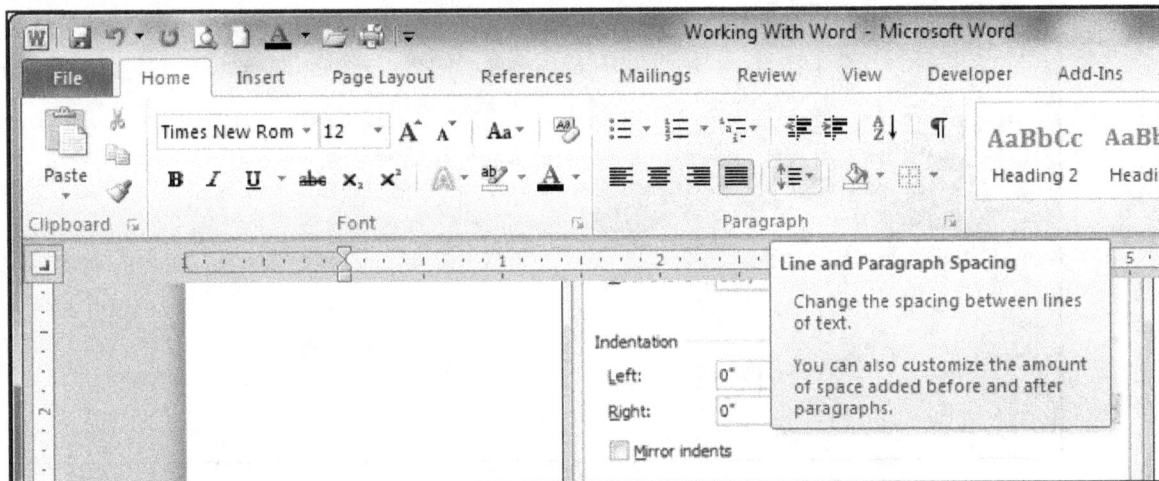

Figure 6. Using the Paragraph group to change line and paragraph spacing

If you find the ribbon distracting, you can collapse (minimize) it by double clicking on any of the tabs except the File tab. When you double click on any other tab, you will have a larger work area, and the ribbon will still be available when you need it. Just click once on any tab to see the ribbon, which will now float atop your document. When you click in the document again, the ribbon will disappear. If you want to restore the ribbon, double click on a tab again. The following screen shot (Figure 7) shows Word 2010 with the ribbon collapsed.

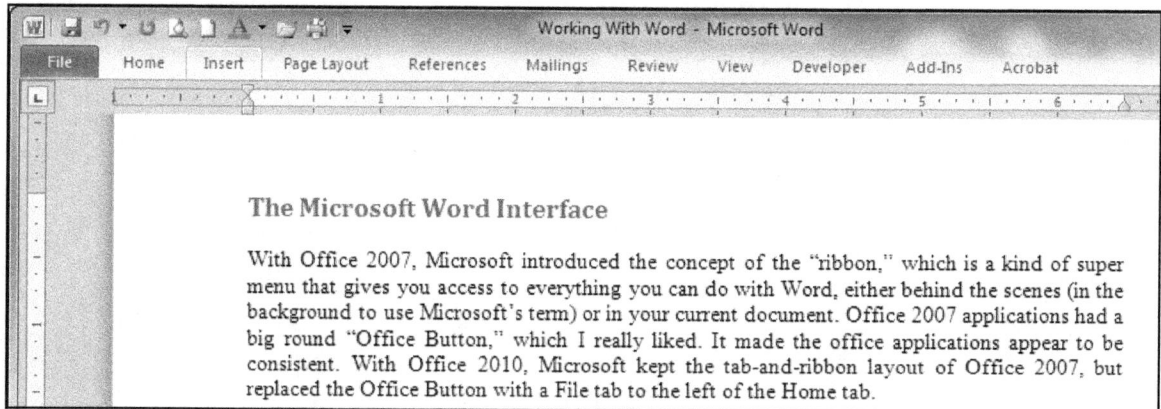

Figure 7. Collapse the ribbon by double clicking on any tab except the File tab.

Throughout the remainder of this book, the ribbon is always maximized so readers can see exactly how to use the various options available. I use a shortcut way to refer to commands and features of Word that you can access via the ribbon. I use **Tab > Ribbon > Group > Command** as a way to describe an action. I also use boldface type consistently when you should click on a command, or access a particular group. This will make it easier for us to communicate and for you to follow my instructions. For example, if you need to access the Page Setup dialog, which we will discuss in detail when we get to page headers, I could tell you to click on the Page Layout tab and locate the Page Setup group and then to find the Launch Page Setup dialog icon at the bottom right corner of the group. However, is simpler and clearer to write **Page Layout > Page Setup > Launch Page Setup dialog** (see Figure 8).

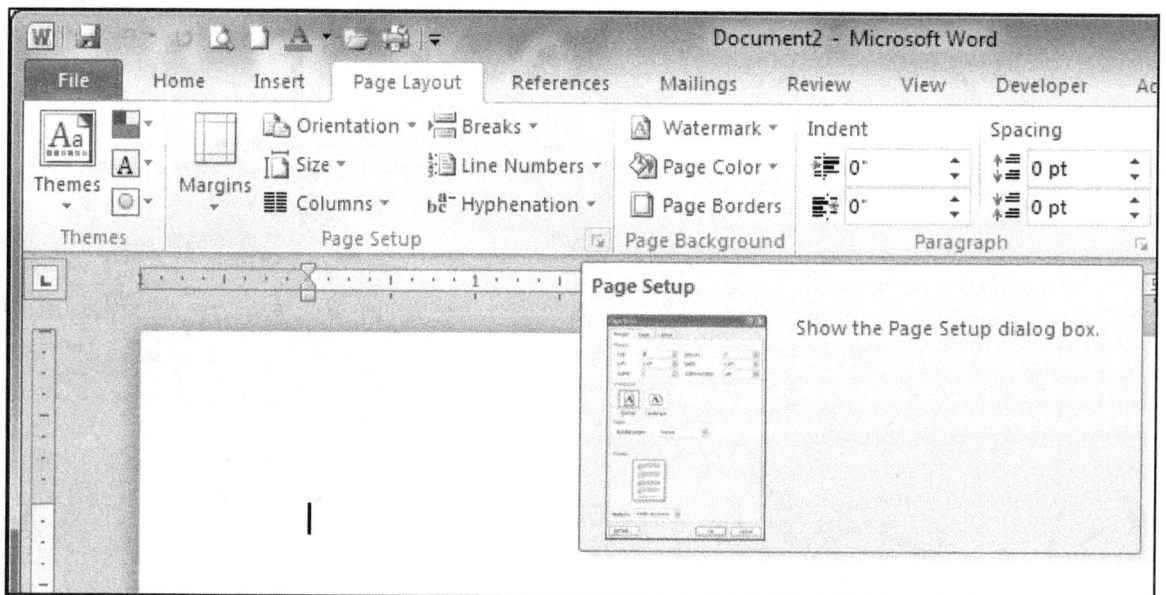

Figure8. A preview of the Page Setup dialog box

Remember if you are not sure what a button or icon will do when you click on it, you can pause the mouse pointer over it for a description or preview.

XML: A New File Format

Microsoft introduced a new file format with Office 2007. Word documents in versions 2007, 2010, and 2011 are saved by default in an XML-based format, and the file extension for Word documents in those versions is *.docx, rather than *.doc, as it is for previous versions of Word. XML stands for extensible markup language, and produces files that are smaller than those from the previous versions, and which are generally more compatible with other applications. HTML (hypertext markup language) is a subset of XML.

The new file type is generally a positive attribute, but problems may arise with certain electronic mail servers and web sites (including some online classrooms) that mistakenly recognize XML files as archive or script files rather than documents, and refuse to attach or download them as a result of that misidentification, or cause them to be downloaded as ZIP files rather than documents. Another problem is that Word embeds XML into the document so that if you try to cut and paste a formatted document into an HTML text box, such as an online classroom discussion forum, you will most likely lose your formatting or have it badly mangled in the translation. HTML and word processing programs treat spacing and tabs quite differently, and it is almost impossible to achieve a proper hanging indent in HTML. For this reason, you may decide to use Notepad or another simple text editor for your discussion posts, or you may simply want to save the Word document as plain text before pasting the contents into the discussion. To save the file as a text document, select **File** > **Save As** and select Plain Text as the format.

If you have problems sending and receiving *.docx files, you can save the file in "compatibility version," which will convert it to the older *.doc format. This format will make it possible for users of earlier versions of Word from 1997 to 2003 to open and edit your document.

To save your file in the earlier *.doc format, simply select **File** > **Save As** and specify Word 97–2003 Document as the file type (see Figure 9, below).

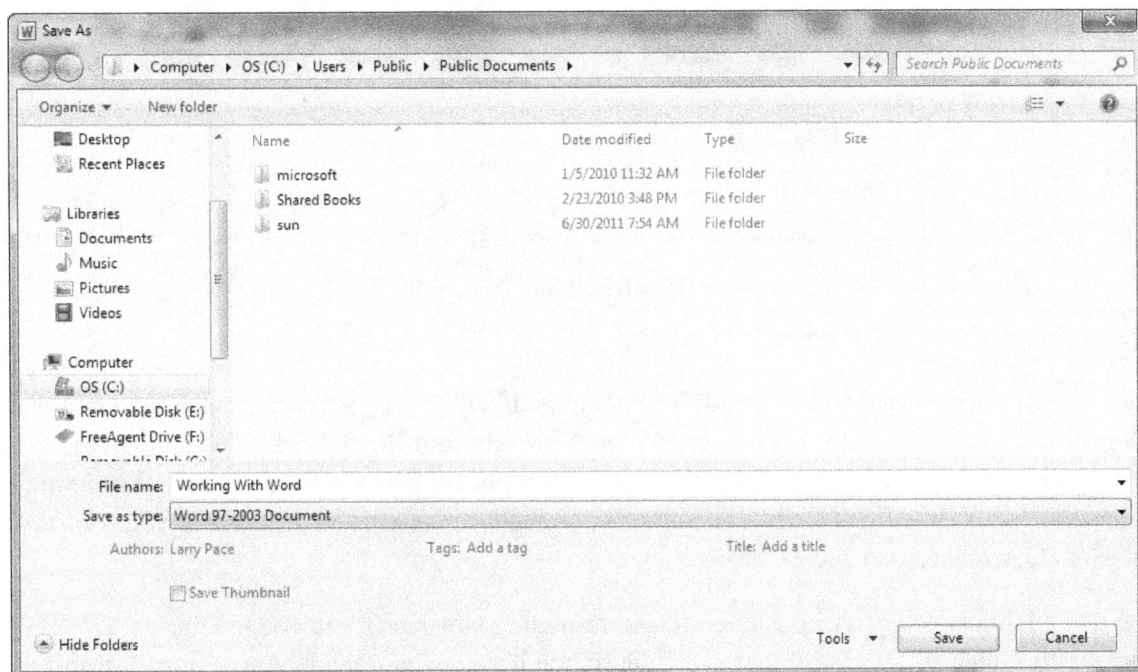

Figure 9. Saving a Word document in "compatibility" form

If you do not have Word 2007, 2010, or 2011, you can download a free "compatibility pack" from Microsoft that will allow you to open and edit files in the newer format with earlier versions of Word:

http://www.microsoft.com/download/en/details.aspx?displaylang=en&id=3

The File Tab: Getting to the "Backstage View

The File tab works differently from the other tabs, and in a way similar to the Office button in Word 2007. Clicking there brings up what Microsoft calls the "backstage view" of your document. You can open, close, save, and print documents from the File tab (see Figure 10). You can also access additional Word options.

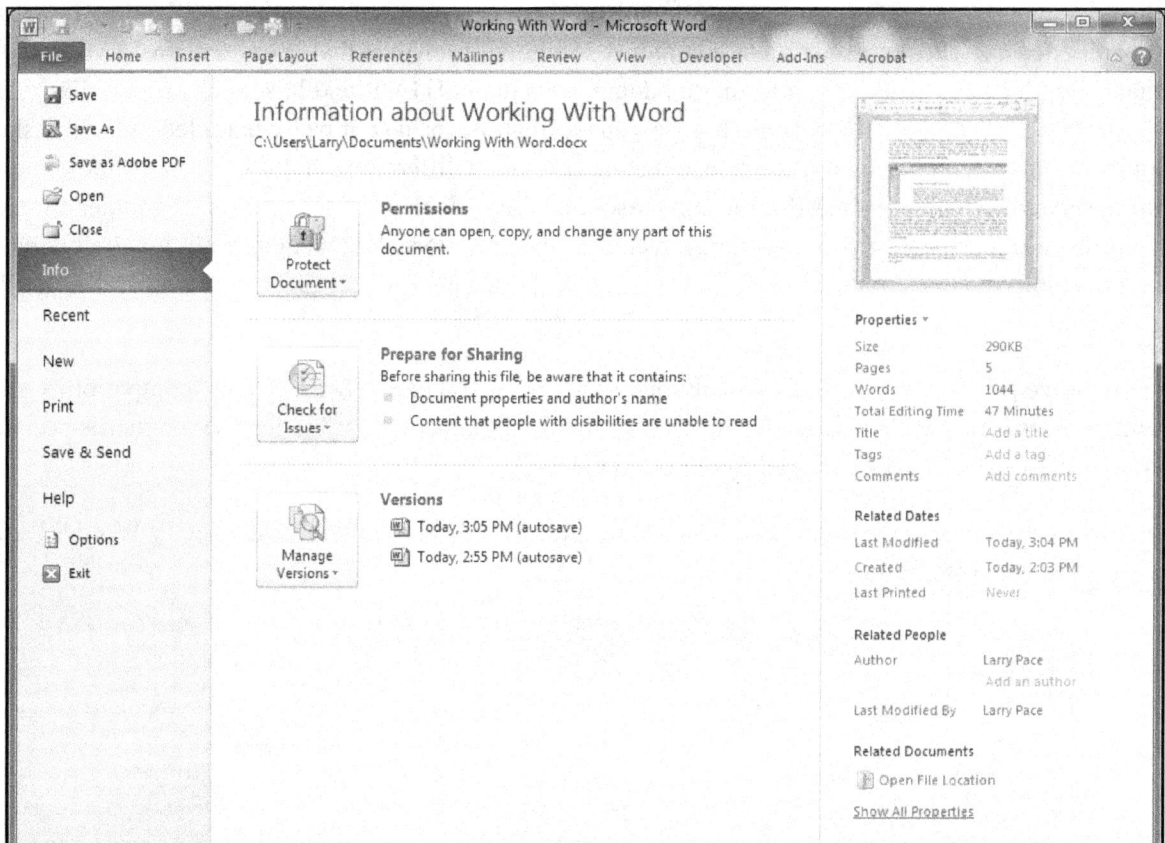

Figure 10. Microsoft calls this the "backstage view."

Customizing the Quick Access Toolbar

As mentioned above, my Quick Access Toolbar most likely has a few more icons on it than yours does. I put the Save File, Open File, Print Preview, Font Color, New File, and Quick Print icons there because I use them often in my work. Here is how to customize the toolbar. Simply click on the little downward-pointing arrow at the right of the toolbar. You will see the most common commands already listed. If the ones you want are not there, click on More Commands (see Figure 11).

Beyond adding new tabs by installing add-ins, accessing new tabs when you use certain features of Word, or putting the Quick Access Toolbar beneath the ribbon if you want it there, you cannot customize the ribbon in any other way except to minimize and restore it, as discussed above. Although this may bother some users, it is not an entirely bad thing, because you also cannot move the ribbon, or even worse, delete it, as you could the menu bar in previous versions of Word.

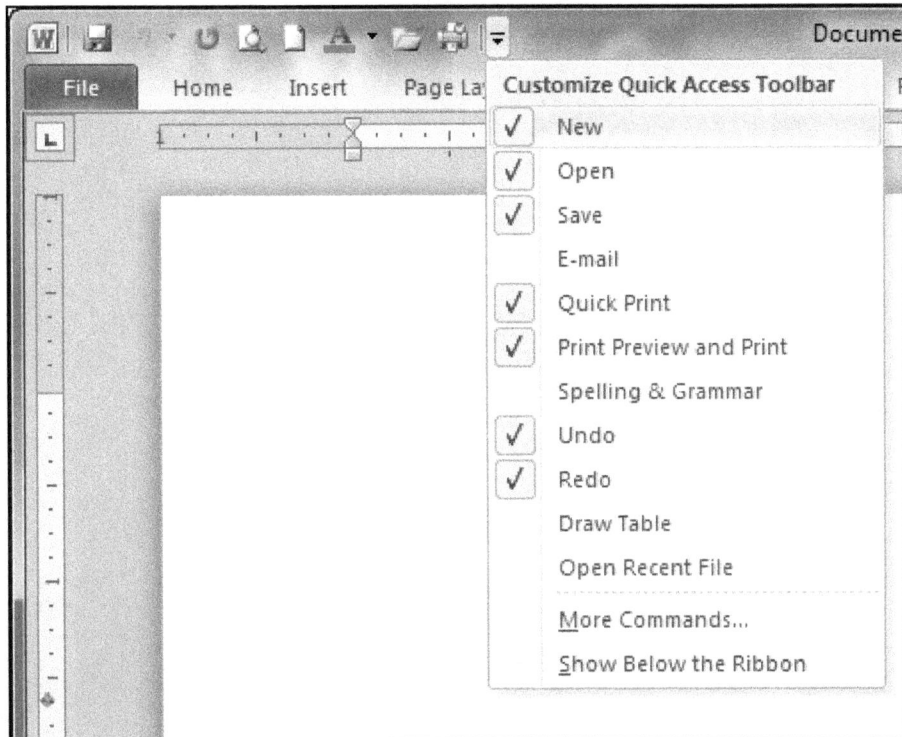

Figure 11. Customizing the Quick Access Toolbar is easy

Looking Ahead

Before progressing to various formatting and writing issues students typically find challenging, we will deal in Chapter 2 with the basics of creating and viewing a document.

Chapter 2—Creating and Viewing Documents

In my experience, many, if not most, users typically launch Word to create a new blank document, and simply start typing and formatting as they go along. This wastes time because you will have to do the same things repetitively to get the format correct. Word's default features, which are saved in the template file Normal.dotx, are fine for general use, but not at all suited for APA formatting. In addition to opening a new blank document, you can also create a new document from an existing document to save yourself some time. Even better, you can create a document from a document template. In fact, you can create and save your own template file that has all the formatting preset for you so that you do not have to set it up again with each new document. The final chapter of this book provides an explanation of how to create, save, and use a template file, which will speed up, streamline, and simplify your document creation. Moreover, your template can assure you of proper APA formatting for all your papers.

Like most typical users, you probably have only scratched the surface of Word's automated features. Although a few of my students seem to master APA style over the course of a class or two, most do not, and even fewer are able to use Word's features effectively.

Creating a Document From Another Document

If you have a paper that you want to use as the basis for a new document, you can select **File** > **New** > **New** from existing (See Figure 12). The three dots (technically known as *ellipsis points*) at the end mean that when you click here, another dialog box will open.

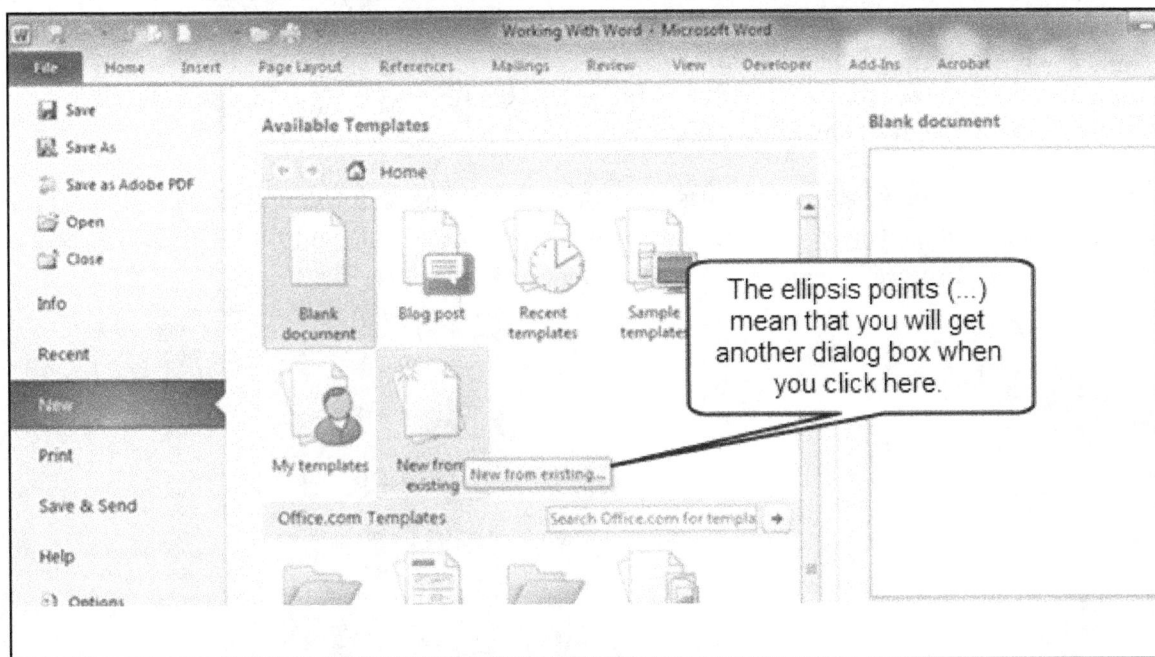

Figure 12. Creating a document from another document

The next dialog box is displayed below (Figure 13). Click New from existing. See that the Title Bar now presents the title "New from Existing Document." Now, simply navigate to the appropriate document and click to select it and then click Create New. This will create a copy of the original document.

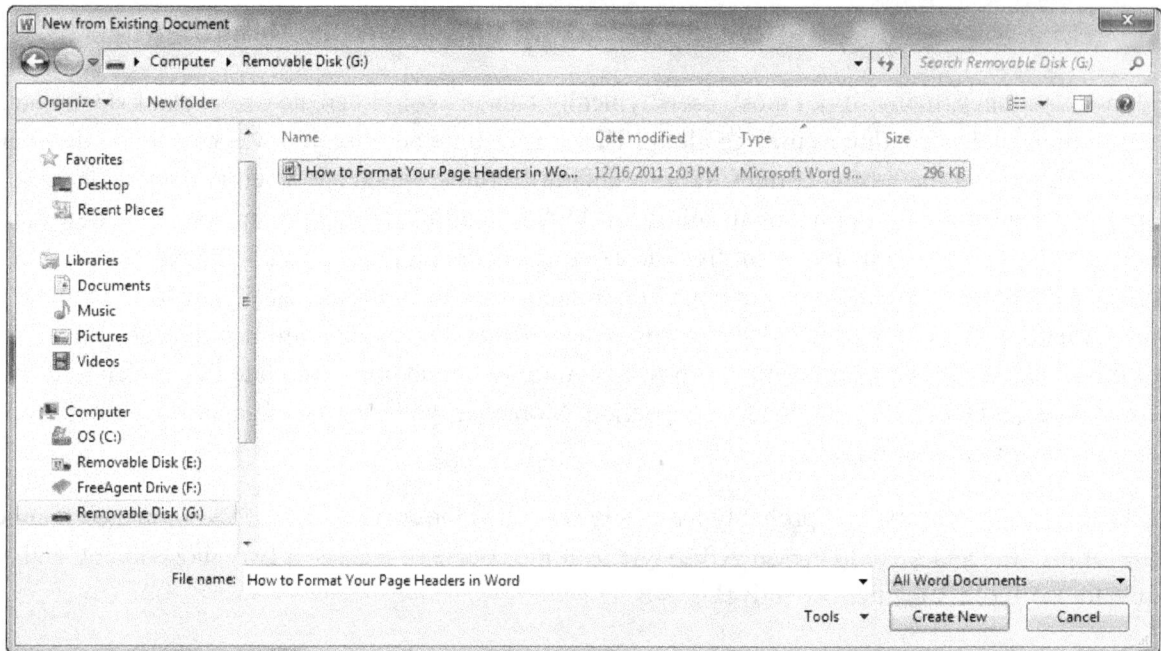

Figure 13. Finding an existing document to use as the basis for a new document

Your new document will be a copy of the original document. Word labeled mine Document 5, but you can save yours with any name you like. You will have to edit the document to remove the content, but all the styles, spacing, fonts, margins, and other features you have set for the existing document will apply to the new one. This is a bit of an advantage, but not a big one, as you could just as easily open the existing document and save it with a new name to accomplish the same effect.

Creating a Document From a Template

Templates are files on which you can base new documents. The template will allow you to get the format you want without additional changes. There are many templates available with Word 2010. To see a list, you can click on **File** > **New**. A screen like the following will appear (Figure 14).

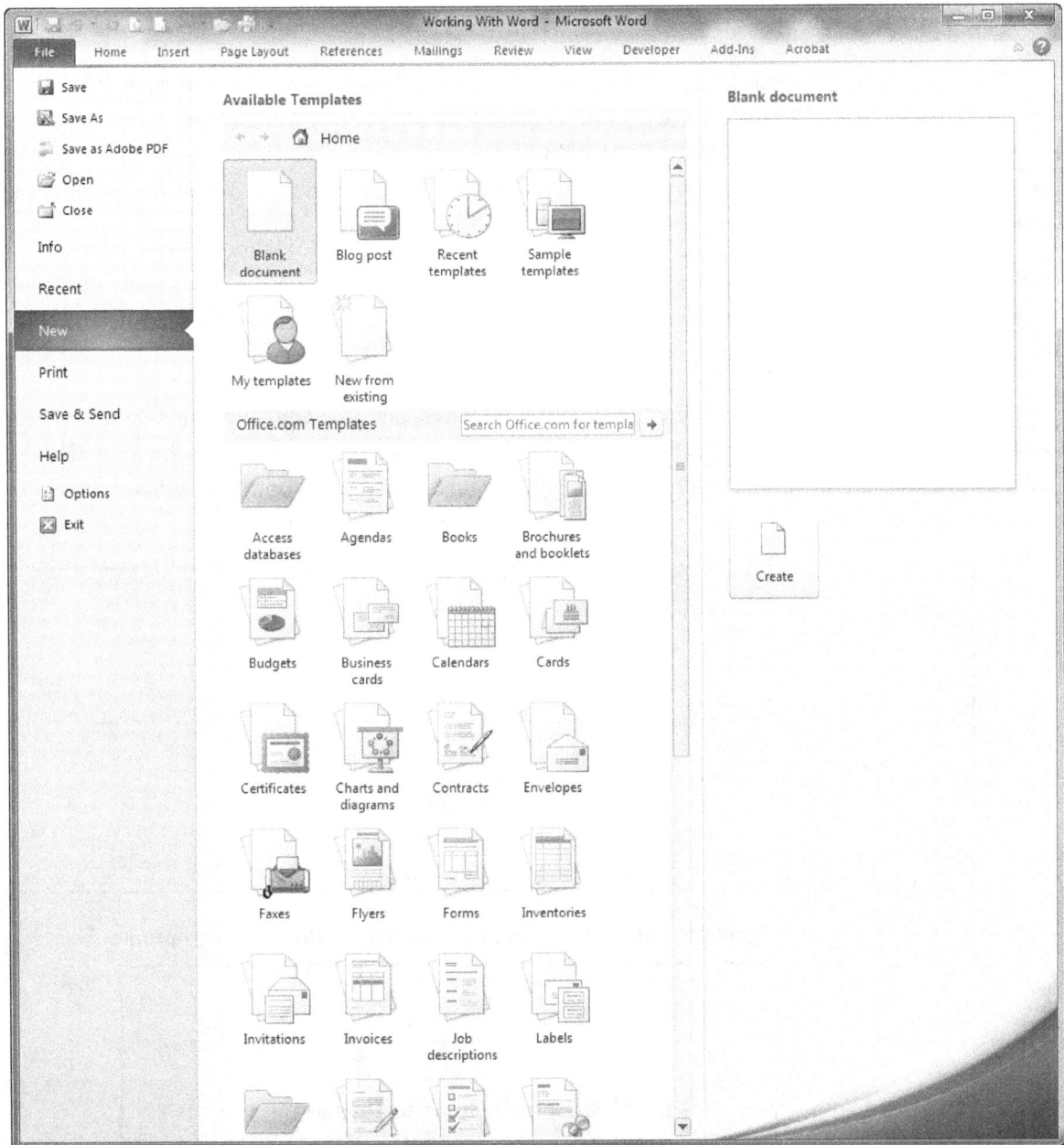

Figure 14. Accessing predefined templates

Templates make it easy to produce various kinds of documents. The ones Microsoft provides are professionally developed, and many of them are stunning. Unfortunately, for students, there is not an APA-compliant Microsoft Word template, but you can create one of your own if you like, and use it for all your papers. You will find many software programs and web sites that purport to provide correct APA style, but in my experience, these are not reliable, especially when it comes to the newest version of APA style. We will discuss the features available via the References tab a little later, and you will find that the bibliographic tools in Word 2010 provide APA 6th edition formatting options. As you will learn later in this book, using this tool does not guarantee correct formatting. You still have to know APA style for the tool to work properly.

After we discuss more of the basics of formatting and writing your papers, I will show you how to create and use your own APA style template in the final chapter of this book. For now, let us continue with our broad overview of Word and its features.

Viewing Your Document

Word provides five different document views. To see the different types, click on **View** > **Document Views**. You may prefer to work in the Outline view while you are drafting your document and in the Print Layout when you are formatting it. I am using the Print Layout throughout this book. The Print Layout is a WYSIWYG (What You See is What You Get) version of (pretty much) what your document will look like when it is printed or when someone else views it.

You can show and hide different aspects of your document. For example, I always show the Ruler (see Figure 15) because it makes it easier to set tabs, indentation, and margins. The Gridlines will not help much unless you are lining up graphics or inserting a drawing, in which case they will be helpful.

You can zoom the view of your document in different ways, and you can customize the zoom features by clicking on the little magnifying class icon (Figure 15). You can also increase or decrease the zoom level by using the slider or clicking on the minus and plus buttons in the Status Bar at the bottom right corner of the screen. In the same area are little shortcuts to the various document views as well (Figure 16).

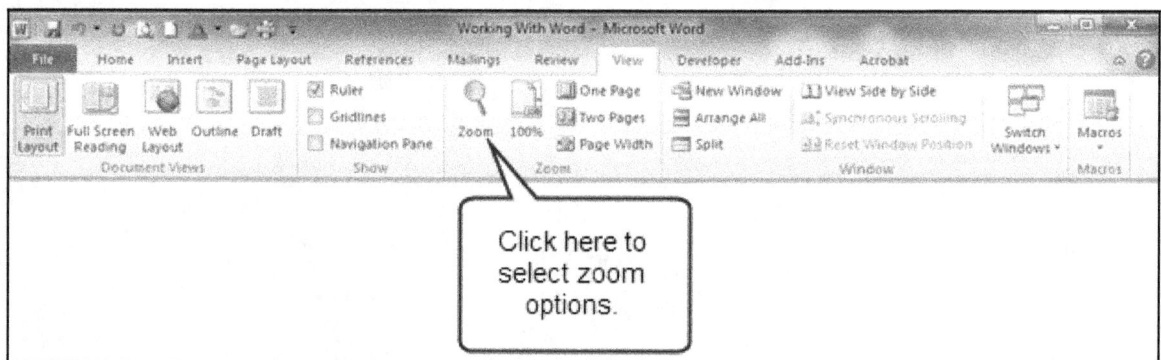

Figure 15. Using the Zoom group to change the zooming options

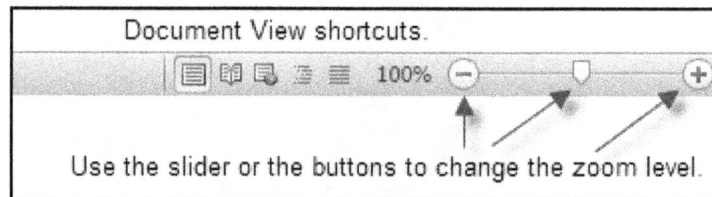

Figure 16. Use this slider or these buttons to increase or decrease the zoom percentage. Note these buttons are at the bottom right corner of the Word interface.

Looking Ahead

In Chapter 3, we will discuss how to modify and use document styles.

Chapter 3—Using and Modifying Styles

Word allows you to specify various styles, including normal text and different levels of headings. The default styles in Word are not APA-friendly, but you can change them easily. Word 2010 defaults to Calibri 11-point font for normal text, and Cambria font for headings, and although these are very nice-looking, they are not acceptable for APA formatting. In APA format, the recommended (and often university-required) font is Times Roman (or Times New Roman) font. The preferred size is 10 or 12 point font, but in my experience, most universities require 12-point font. This font and size should be applied to all the text in your document, including the page headers and numbers. You can specify these in a document template, as we will discuss later, or change them in your current document.

The APA manual also says that you should double space your entire document without extra spacing before or after a paragraph, as we discussed previously. You can change the font and size for both your text and your page headers by using the commands on the Home ribbon (Figure 17), or by launching the Font dialog (see Figure 18).

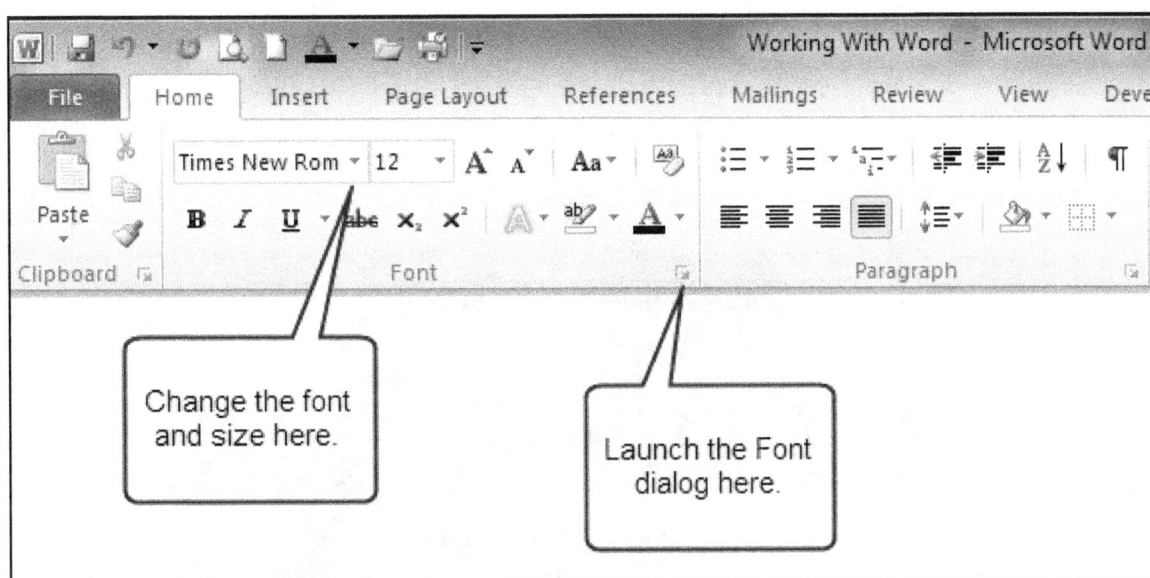

Figure 17. Using the Font group to change font and size and launch the Font dialog box

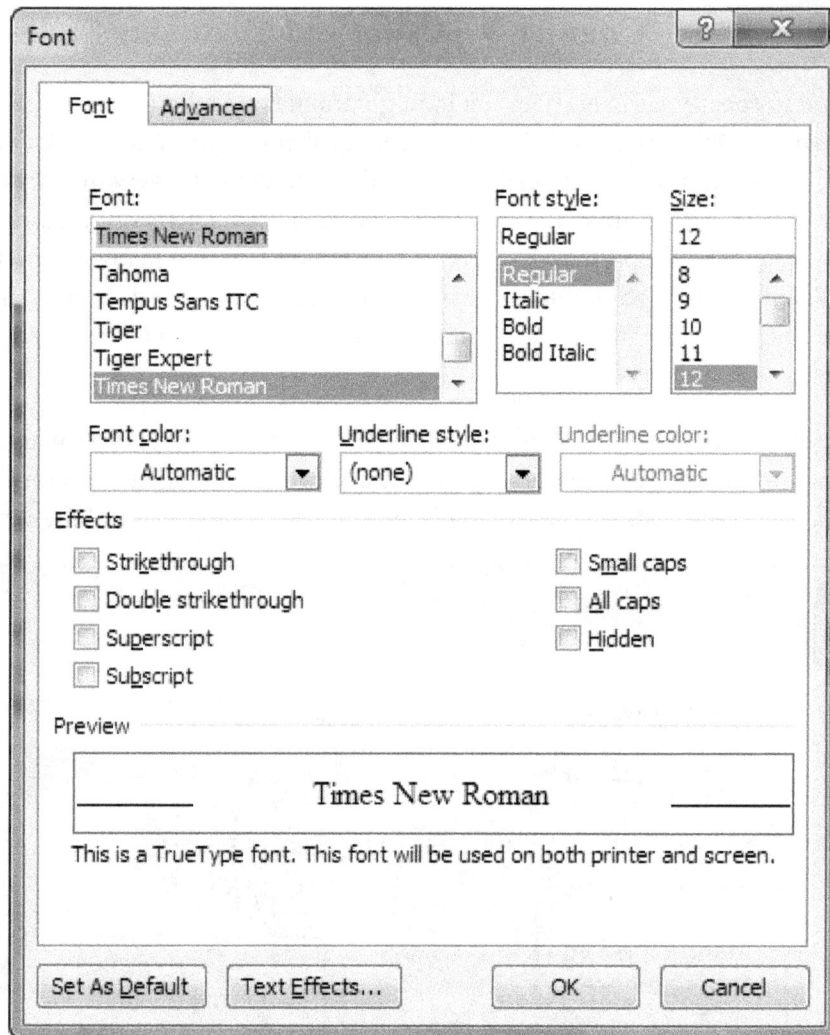

Figure 18. The Font dialog box

As we discussed, in the Paragraph dialog you will find commands for spacing and indentation (see Figure 19). This dialog box also has a tab for setting the options for line and page breaks. The feature to control "widows and orphans" is selected by default. You may also want to check Keep lines together. A widow is a paragraph in a document that has a single line at the beginning of a new page. An orphan is the opposite, a new paragraph that has a single line at the end of a page. Both are considered poor form in page layout.

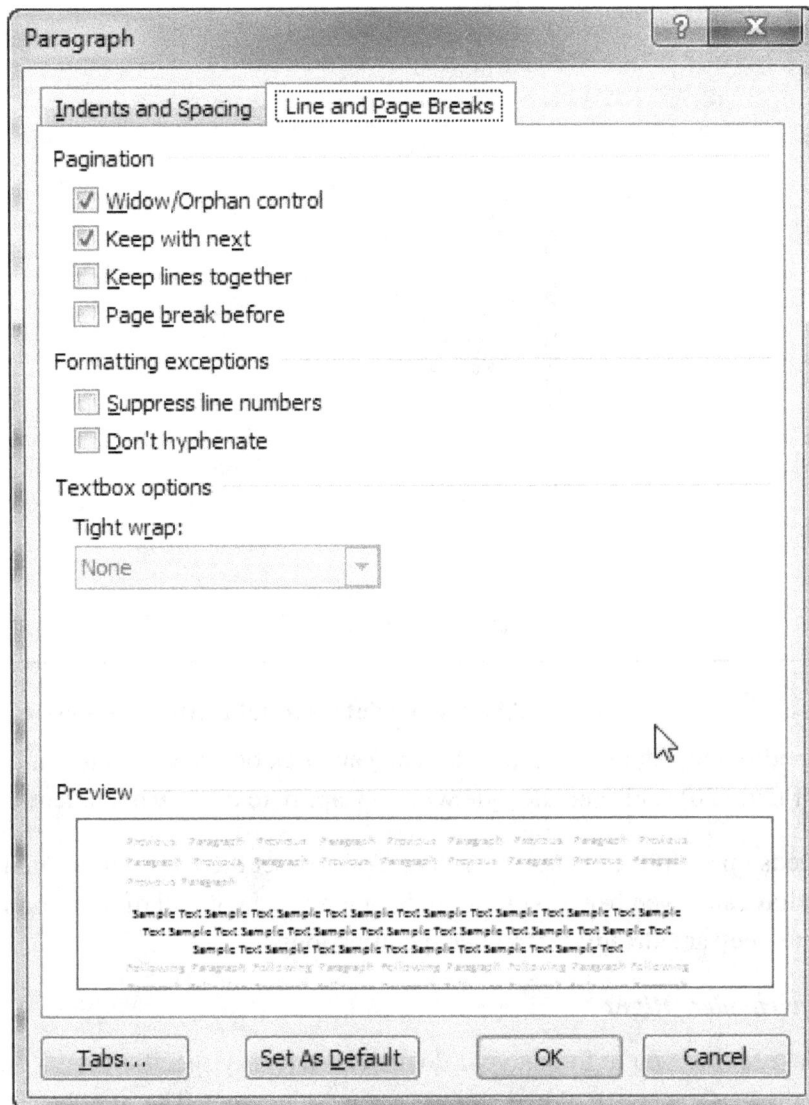

Figure 19. The Paragraph dialog box

After you have set the font and the spacing, you can modify the Normal style to match your new selections in a couple of ways. The simplest is to select the text that is formatted the way you want it to appear, and then right-click on the Normal icon in the Styles group. Click on Update Normal to Match Selection, and all the body text in your document will be updated to match your selected text (see Figure 20). Any new or existing text in your document using this style will also automatically be formatted this way. This includes font, margins, and spacing. You can also select Modify to edit the features of this or any other style.

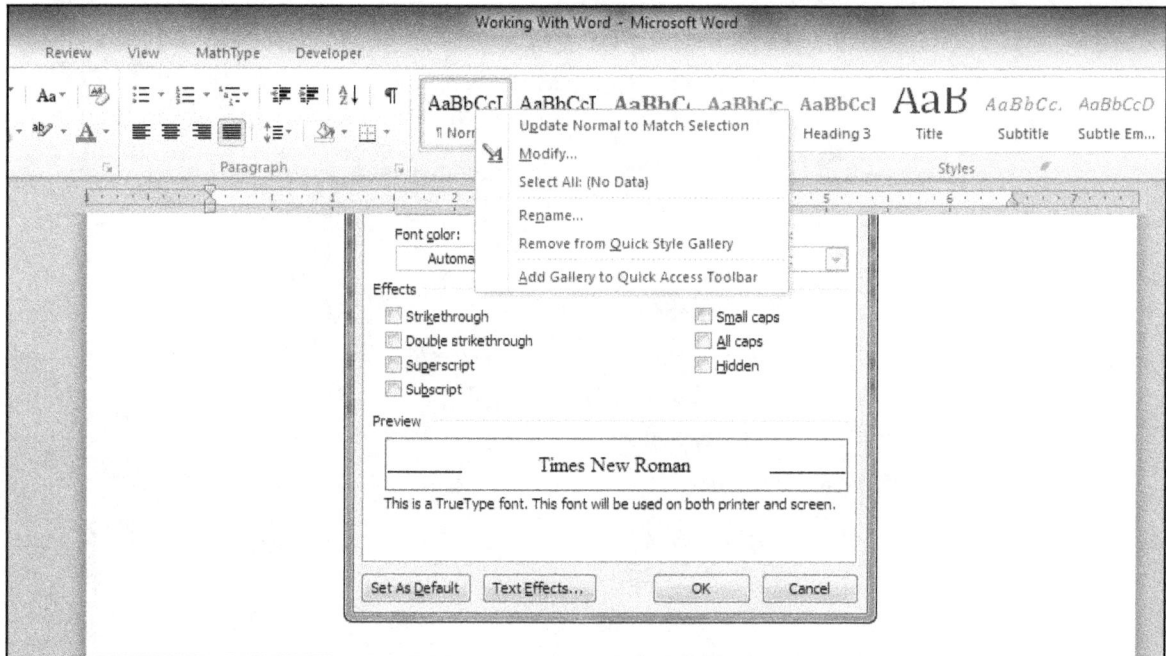

Figure 20. Select "Update Normal to Match Selection"

If you want to modify the default Normal style, you can click on Set as Default at the bottom left corner of the dialog box (see Figure 20). This default style will now apply to all new documents.

Using styles speeds up your document formatting. You can set the styles for normal text, headings, and references by using this feature, and even better, you can build a template with all of these preformatted so that when you open the template, they are already set to your specifications.

Getting the Page Headers Right

The APA manual requires you to format your document in a very specific way. You need a page header and the page number in the header section of every page of your document. The page header consists of what is known as the "Running head" at the left margin and the page number at the right margin. "Running head" (without the quotes, obviously) literally should be typed on page 1, followed by a colon, a single space, and then a condensed title in ALL CAPS. As we discuss later, if your full title is brief, you can use the entire title in the running head. On all other pages, "Running head" is omitted, but the condensed title or the brief full title in all caps still appears at the left margin. This requirement is a new one with the sixth edition of the APA manual, and getting this right is the single biggest problem students have with formatting their papers.

According to the APA manual, you should not type the page headers and numbers repeatedly in your document (APA, 2010, p. 230), though many students do that simply because they cannot figure out how to format the page header differently on the first page. To accomplish this, go to Page Layout > Page Setup, and click the icon to launch the Page Setup dialog (Figure 21). Click on the Layout tab and you can check the box to get a different header on the first page.

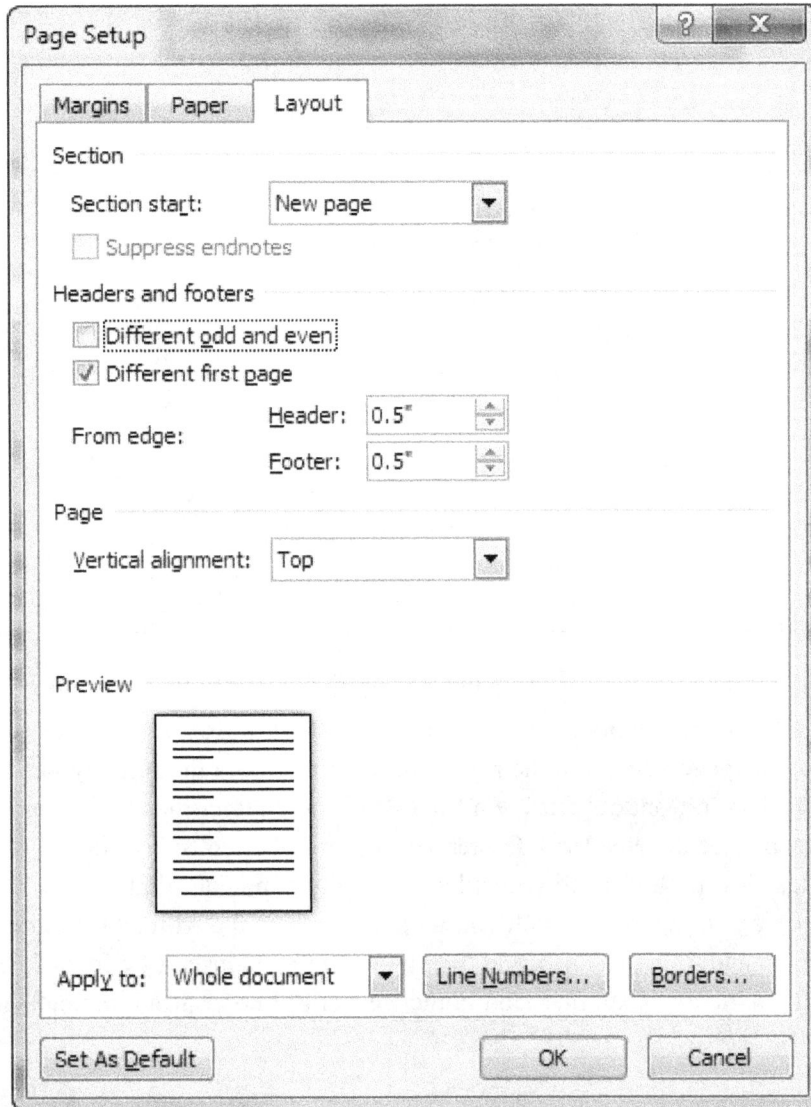

Figure 21. The Page Setup dialog box

Now, click OK to close the dialog box. There are a couple of ways to get into the page header section for page 1. The most direct way is just to place the mouse in the header section and double click (see Figure 22).

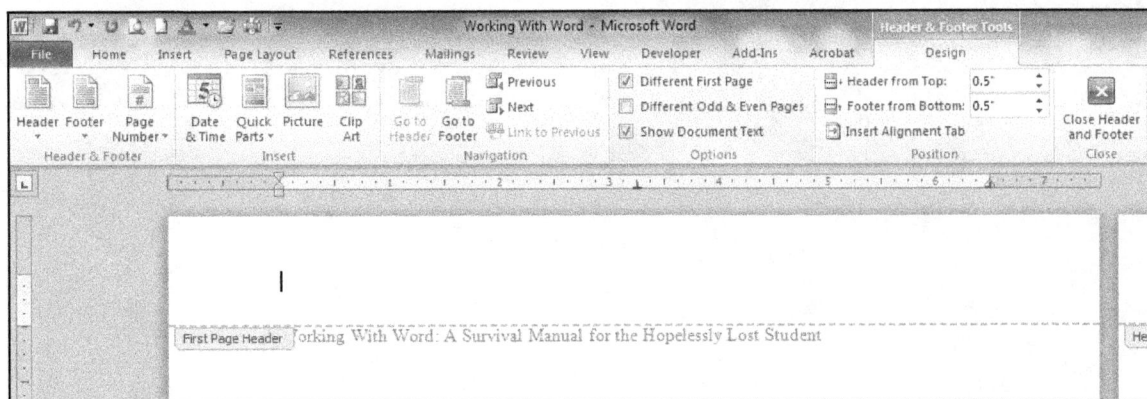

Figure 22. Double click in the header section to access the Header & Footer Tools.

You can also select **Insert** > **Header & Footer** > **Header** to edit the header (see Figure 23), but this involves more steps than clicking in the header section.

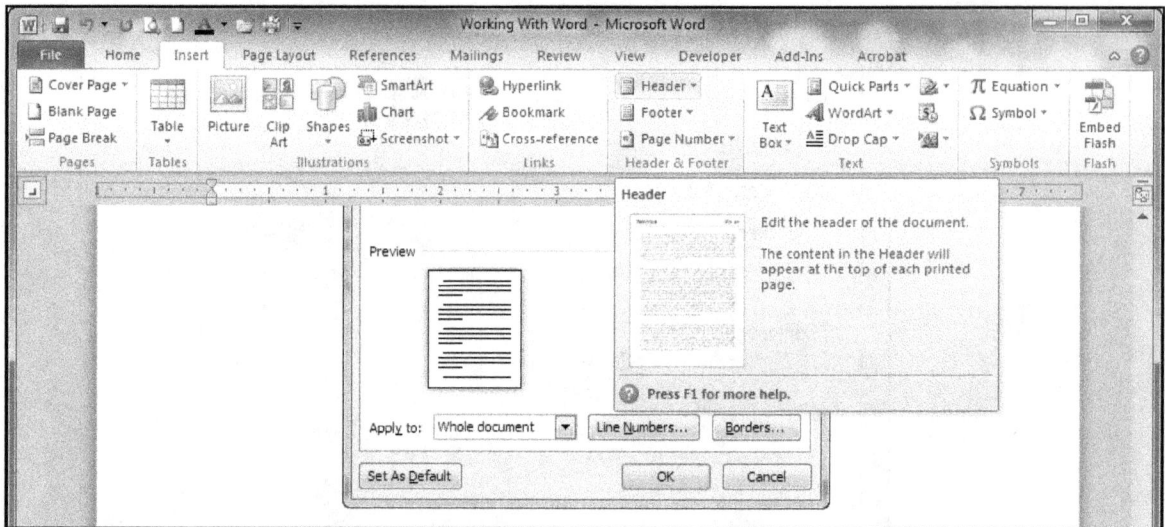

Figure 23. Using the Header & Footer group to edit the header

When you are in the header section, you now have access to the Header & Footer Tools with a Design tab that allows you to add the page number at the right margin after typing the running head at the left margin. You can also just check the box in front of "Different First Page" here rather than using the Page Setup menu. After typing the header, you can close the Header & Footer Tools or more directly just double click in the document to close the menu. The header is preformatted with a left margin that matches that of your document, a center tab (which you will not need), and a right tab (which you will need). Type the words "Running head" (omitting the quotes), followed by a colon and a single space, and then type your condensed title in ALL CAPS. Tab over to the right margin, and click on the Page Number icon in the Header & Footer group. Select Current Position and then select Plain Number (see Figure 24).

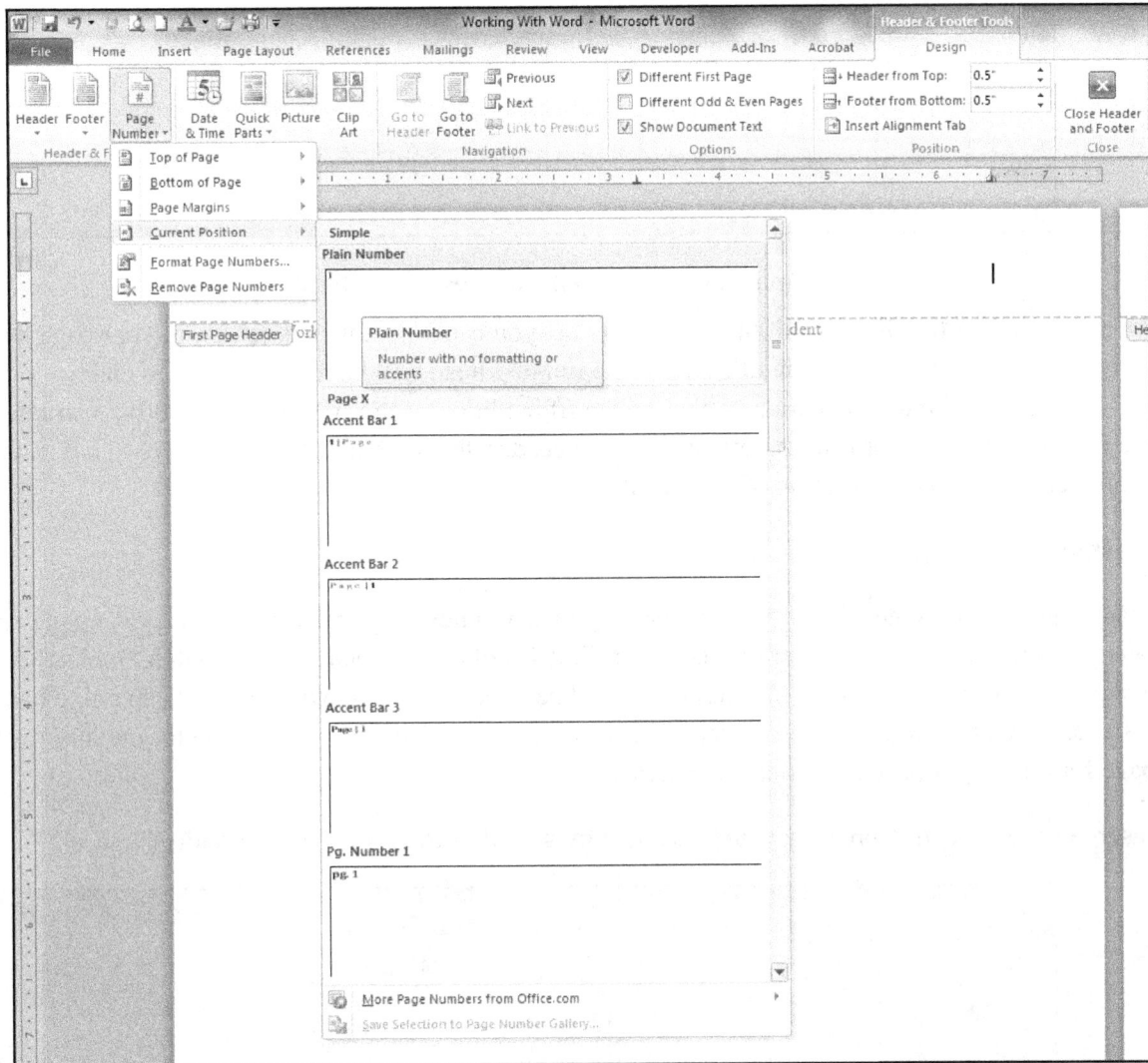

Figure 24. APA says to use the automated features of your word processing program to insert the page numbers.

Here is the correctly formatted page header for page 1 (Figure 25). Note that the h in "head" should not be capitalized. The majority of students miss this!

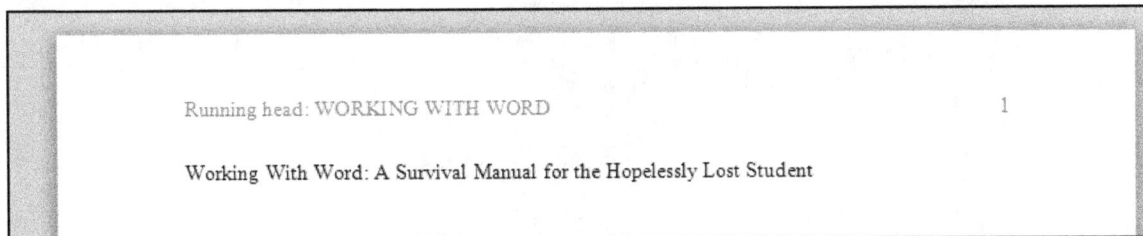

Running head: WORKING WITH WORD   1

Working With Word: A Survival Manual for the Hopelessly Lost Student

Figure 25. The correctly formatted page header for page 1

Because we specified a different page header on page 1, there are no headers on the other pages. Just repeat the process you used before, and double click in the page header section of page 2. Type the condensed title in ALL CAPS without the words "Running head," and then tab over to the right margin and insert the page number as shown above. Here is the correctly formatted page header for page 2 and all subsequent pages (Figure 26).

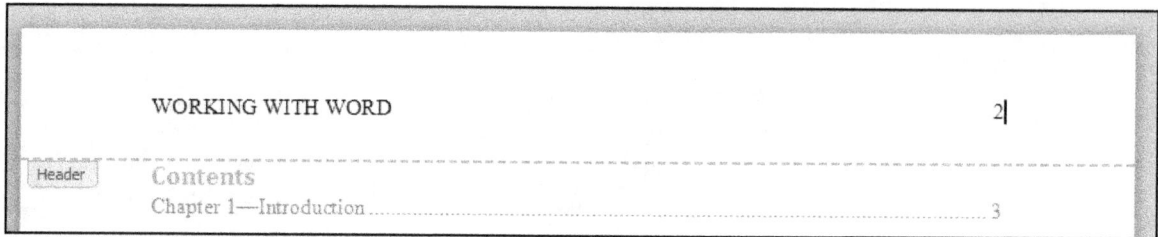

Figure 26. The correctly formatted page header for page 2

As mentioned earlier, if your full title is a short one, you can repeat the entire title in your page headers. If the title is long, you should condense the title so that the running head will be no more than 50 characters in length, including spacing and punctuation. Although the fifth edition of the APA manual (2001) instructed writers to use the first two or three words of the title in the page header, the sixth edition (2010) says to use a standalone shortened (as necessary) version of the full title.

Starting a New Page

Many students press the <**Enter**> key repeatedly to start a new page after typing the cover page or abstract and when they are ready to type their reference list. This is not a good idea, even though it "looks right," because when your document is edited, the pagination will be altered, and you will have to keep going back to adjust it. Instead, start a new page for the abstract (if you are using an abstract), a new page for the introduction, and a new page for the reference list by using page breaks.

Insert a page or section break in your document by selecting **Page Layout** > **Breaks** (Figure 27).

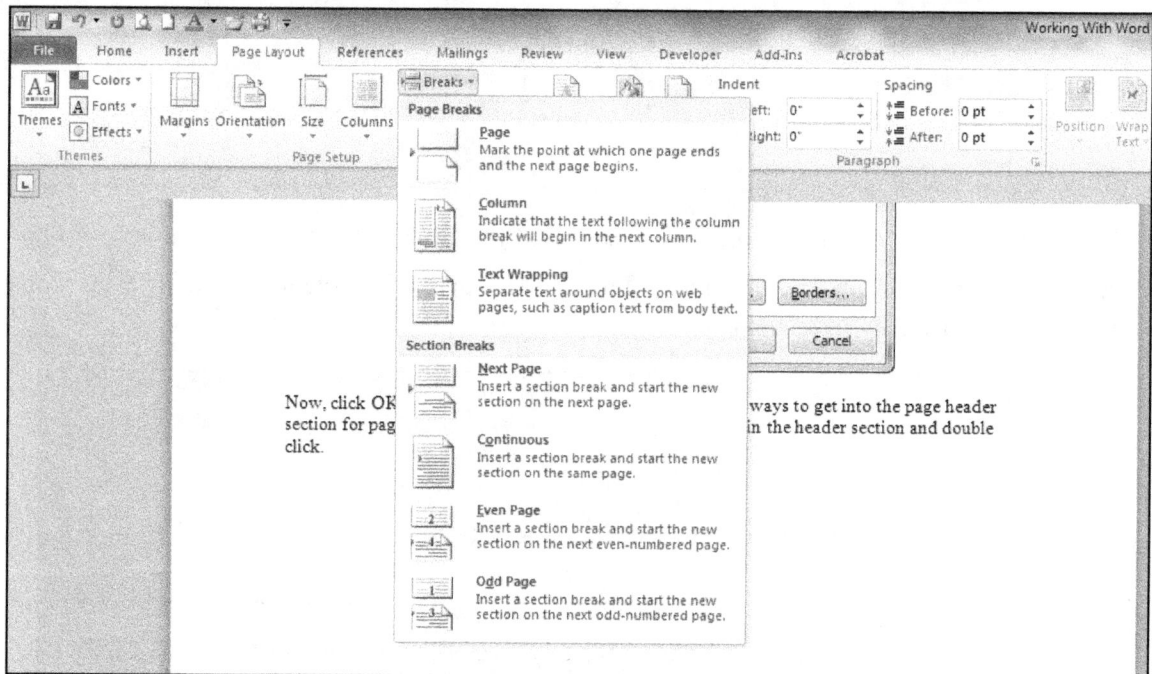

Figure 27. Using the Page Setup group to insert a page break

A more direct way to insert a page break is to use the keyboard shortcut of pressing <**Ctrl**> + <**Enter**>. With a page break inserted, any changes to your document that increase or decrease the number of pages will not change the formatting of pages after the break.

About Headings

Now that you know how your page headers should be formatted (along with how to do it), and where to find the layout options for spacing, let us discuss styles in greater depth. Word comes with a variety of predefined styles, and you can add others as well as modify the default styles. If you make these changes to the Normal.dotx template, all your new documents will use those styles. However, you can also make these changes to your current document. As I mentioned earlier, you can also create a template of your own that has all the styles you need for your APA formatted papers.

The APA manual (2010) is very specific about what should appear in boldface and what should not. APA does not consider the repeated title that precedes the introduction, the word Abstract, or the word References to be headings. Instead, these are considered titles of document sections and should be centered at the top of their respective pages, and should be in title case, but not in boldface. Title case in APA style means you should capitalize all major words and any word of four or more letters, regardless of the part of speech. The first word should always be capitalized, and you should always capitalize the first word after a colon or a dash in a title. Do not capitalize short connecting words like a, an, the, but, and or, unless these words are the first word of the title, or the first word after a colon or a dash. Word will object when you try to capitalize words like from and between, but the APA manual says to capitalize ANY word of four or more letters.

APA format recognizes five different levels of heading. All but the last of these levels should be in boldface. Here are the five levels (APA, 2010, p. 62).

First Level of Heading (on a separate line)

Second Level of Heading (on a separate line)

Third level of heading. Text follows here.

    Fourth level of heading. Text follows here.

    Fifth level of heading. Text follows here.

Like the title on the cover page, which is repeated before the introduction, the first two levels of heading should be in title case. The Level 1 heading should be centered, and in boldface. The Level 2 heading should be flush with the left margin and should be in boldface. Level 1 and Level 2 headings should not be followed by any punctuation, and should appear on a separate line from the text. The headings at Levels 3–5 should not be in title case. These should be indented and followed by a period. The first letter of the word should be in uppercase, and the remaining words should be in lowercase (unless they are proper nouns, which should always be capitalized).

For student papers, two levels of headings are generally sufficient. You can set the Heading 1 style to match the APA Level 1 heading, and whenever you need it, just click **Home** > **Styles** > **Heading 1**. You can do the same thing for the second heading level. This will save time and ensure consistency. You should not use Level 2 headings unless you have two or more subsections for which you want to have headings beneath a Level 1 heading.

Say we want to modify the Heading 1 style to match APA style. First, format your Level 1 heading as shown above, and then select it. Now, go to **Home** > **Styles**, and locate Heading 1. Right-click there and then click on Update Heading 1 to Match Selection (See Figure 28). Now, for this document and any other documents created from it, the Level 1 heading will be in APA style. You can do the same thing for Level 2 and other levels of headings if you like.

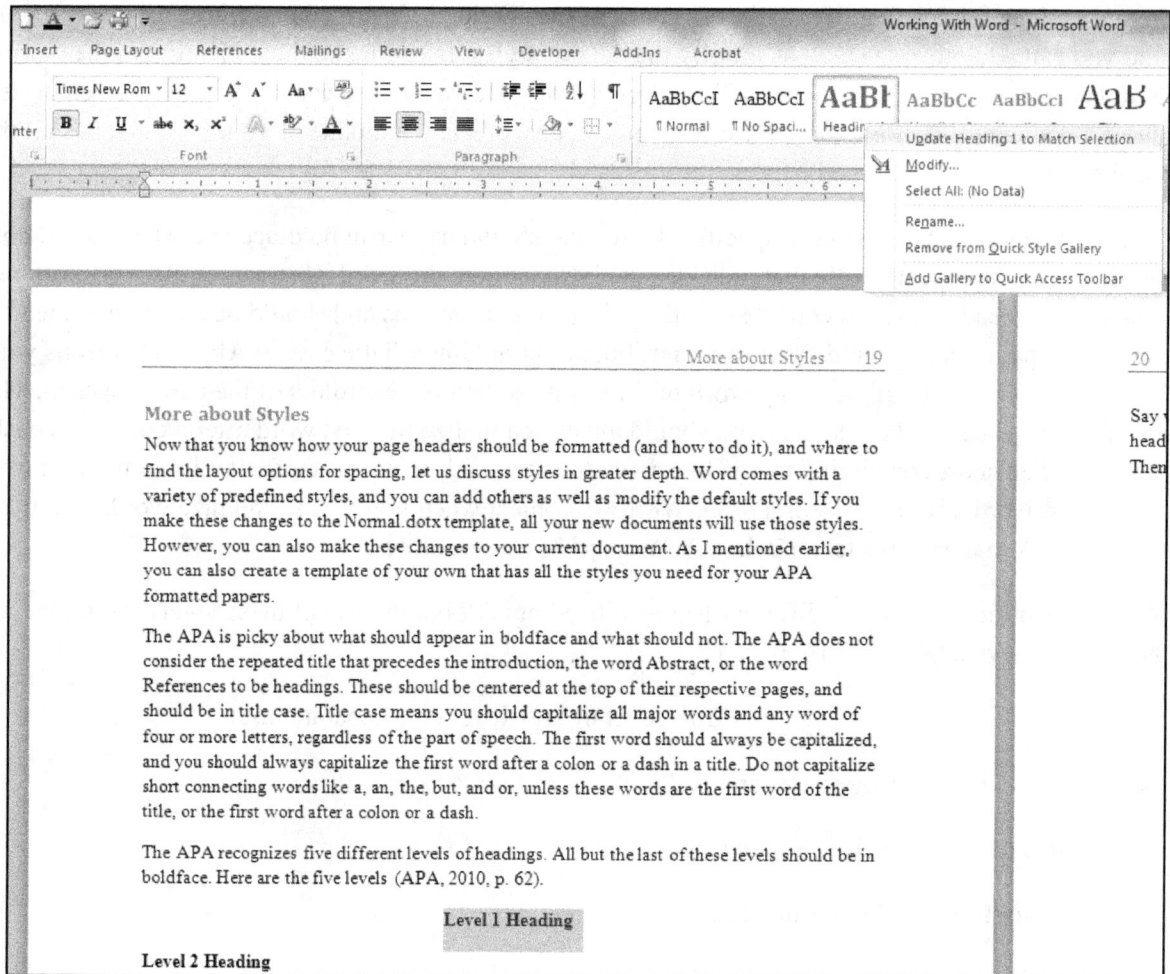

Figure 28. Changing the Heading 1 style to match APA style

Margins and Indentation

As with all other formatting standards, APA style has strict rules for margins and indentation. The APA manual says to use 1-inch margins for the top, bottom, left, and right margins of the document. Many students use the space bar to indent their paragraphs, but that is not what you should do. You should use the <**Tab**> key to insert a one-half inch indentation, which is what the APA manual says to use.

Although you can use the Paragraph dialog to change margins, as we discussed above, you can more easily use the sliders in the Ruler to modify the indentation. This is the most direct way. If you want all new paragraphs to be indented one-half inch, you can simply grab the top (downward pointing) slider at the left margin, and drag it one-half inch to the right. Here is what that looks like (Figure 29).

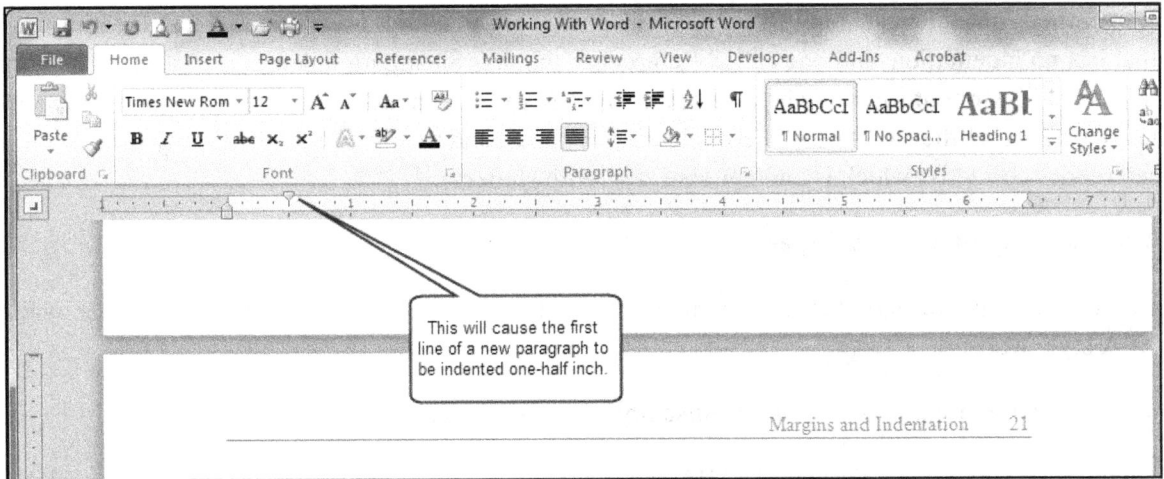

Figure 29. Use the slider to indent paragraphs one-half inch

In your reference list, you need to use a hanging indent. The first line of the reference list entry needs to be flush with the left margin. The second and any subsequent lines of the same reference should be indented one-half inch. Some students use spacing to accomplish this effect, too, but the hanging indent is more effective. Just go to the ruler and drag the upward pointing slider at the left margin ½ inch to the right (Figure 30).

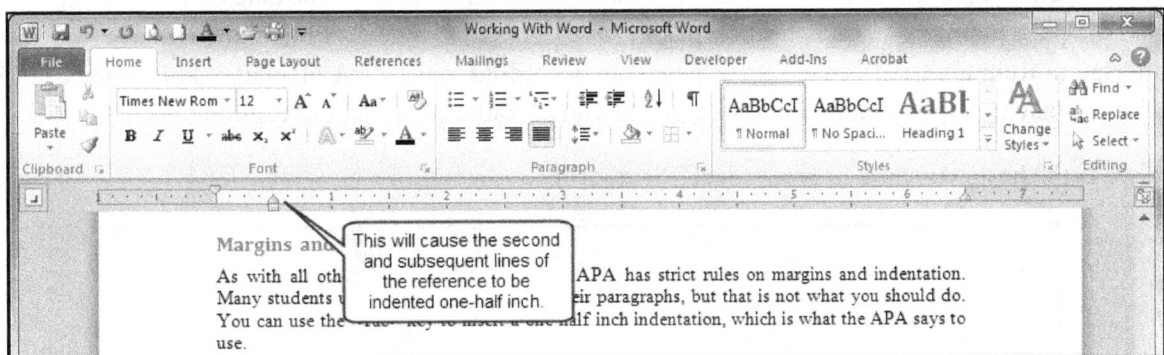

Figure 31. Use the slider to insert a hanging indent

Direct quotes of 40 or more words should be set off as blocks, and should not be enclosed in quotation marks. The first line should be indented the same amount as a paragraph, and all subsequent lines should also be indented the same amount. If there is a new paragraph in the quoted material, it should be indented an additional ½ inch. Quotes of fewer than 40 words should be typed "inline" in the text and should be enclosed in quotation marks.

The APA manual says not to indent the abstract. The abstract should be a single block paragraph that provides a succinct summary of the entire paper. Generally, abstracts should be from 100 to 250 words in length. The abstract is not an introduction or overview. If you are using an abstract (check with your instructor to see whether you should), the abstract should appear alone on page 2. Remember the word Abstract should be centered at the top of the page and should not be in boldface type.

At the top of page 3 (or page 2 if you are not using an abstract), repeat the full title from the cover page. This repeated title should match the one on the cover page and should not be in boldface. Begin the introduction immediately thereafter. The APA manual says not to label the introduction. The introduction is identified by its position in the paper and not by a label (APA, 2010, p. 63).

Remember you can create new styles for your document, you might want to consider creating one called Abstract that has no indentation, and one called References that has a hanging indent. I will discuss this in more detail later, and illustrate it for you when we build an APA style template in the final chapter of this book. For now, we need to examine the structure of a complete APA paper, and then move on the thorny problem of formatting references correctly, which is another sore spot with students.

The Anatomy of an APA Paper

Below, I describe the structure of a complete APA-style paper. There is also a sample paper available through the APA style web site:

http://www.apastyle.org/manual/related/sample-experiment-paper-1.pdf

I encourage you to view the sample APA paper and study it to see the structure required by APA. In addition, an APA style blog contains many helpful tips and examples:

http://blog.apastyle.org/

Page 1—This is the cover page, which should have the author's name and institutional affiliation, and possibly an author note. For most universities, there are additional requirements for the cover page for student papers, which might include the instructor's name, the course name and number, and the date of submission. The running head and the page number should appear on page 1, as discussed above. As I mentioned, many students capitalize the h in head in Running head" on the cover page, but according to the APA manual, that is incorrect. Many students also mistakenly type "Running header" or "Running Header," instead of "Running head."

Here is the basic structure of page 1 (see Figure 31).

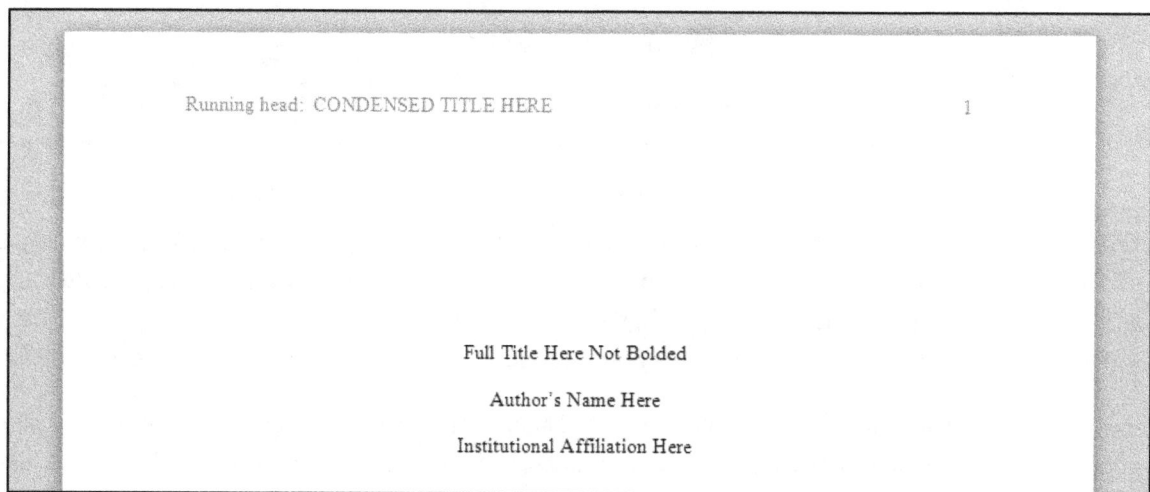

Running head: CONDENSED TITLE HERE   1

Full Title Here Not Bolded

Author's Name Here

Institutional Affiliation Here

Figure 31. The basic structure of page 1, the cover page

Page 2—This is the abstract (if you are using one). The abstract appears alone, and is not indented, as discussed above. Do NOT bold the word Abstract. After typing the abstract, insert a page break (**<Ctrl>** + **<Enter>**) to start the next page.

Here is the basic structure of Page 2 (Figure 32).

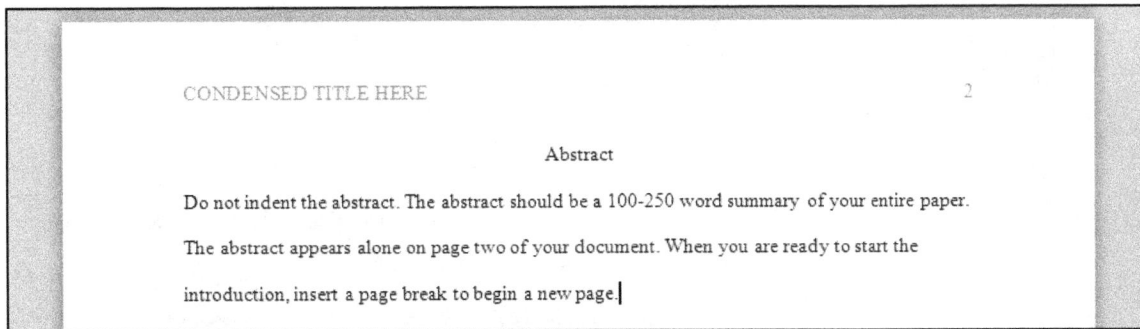

Figure 32. The basic structure of page 2, the abstract page

Page 3—This would be page 2 if you are not using an abstract. Repeat the full title from the cover page, centered, and not in boldface, at the top of the page. Begin the introduction immediately thereafter. All of the body paragraphs of the text should be indented.

Here is the basic structure of page 3 (Figure 33).

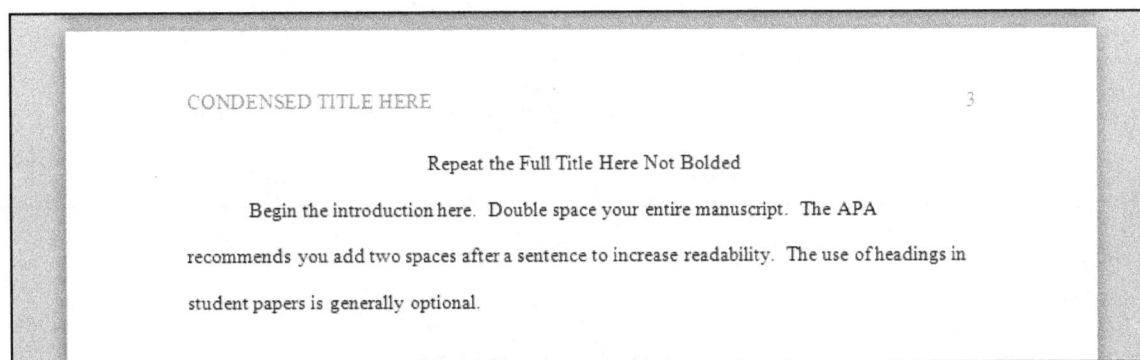

Figure 33. The basic structure of page 3. Begin the introduction immediately after the repeated title.

Subsequent Pages—Depending on the length of your paper, the next several or many pages are the body of your text. Do not start a new page to insert a heading, unless it would appear as an orphan on a line by itself at the bottom of a page. When it is time to start the reference list, insert a page break to start a new page. I will not illustrate the body pages, as they are similar in structure to page 3.

Reference List—The word References should be centered, not in boldface, and there should be no colon or other punctuation after the word References. If you have a single reference, you can use the title Reference. This should not be Works Cited, Bibliography, Sources, or Resources, which many students insist on using. The reference list should have a hanging indent, as we discussed above. Here is the basic structure of the reference list (see Figure 34). I added a reference to the APA manual, a couple of articles, and several textbooks to show you how the reference list should be formatted.

References

American Psychological Association. (2001). *Publication manual of the American Psychological Association* (5th ed.). Washington, DC: Author.

American Psychological Association. (2010). *Publication manual of the American Psychological Association* (6th ed.). Washington, DC: Author.

Durtschi, C., Hillison, W., & Pacini, C. (2004). The effective use of Benford's law to assist in detecting fraud in accounting data. *Journal of Forensic Accounting, 5*, 17-34.

Edwards, N. M. (2007). Student self-grading in social statistics. *College Teaching, 55*(2), 72-76. doi:10.3200/CTCH.55.2.72-76

Lind, D. A., Marchal, W. G., & Wathen, S. A. (2010). *Statistical techniques in business & economics* (14th ed.). Boston, MA: McGraw-Hill Irwin.

Rosnow, R. L., & Rosnow, M. (1986). *Writing papers in psychology: A student guide*. Belmont, CA: Wadsworth.

Figure 34. The basic structure of the reference list

Looking Ahead

With our basic formatting and document structure out of the way, let us look at getting the references right. This thorny subject is the topic of Chapter 4.

Chapter 4—Getting the References Right

APA's formatting rules are confusing, inconsistent, and sometimes contradictory in this area. In this chapter, we address some of these inconsistencies and learn how to get the references right. As a bonus, I show you in Chapter 5 how to use the bibliographic features of Word to insert both in-text citations and correctly-formatted reference lists.

APA style uses author-date format for in-text citations (APA, 2010, p. 174). Use authors' surnames only, followed by the year of publication. In the in-text citation, do not include the month or day, even when they might be part of the reference list entry. When a source has a single author, the in-text citation would take either the form Author (Year), as in Pace (2008), or, in parenthetical citations, (Author, Year), as in (Pace, 2008). If you are citing specific information or quoting directly, you must include a page number or page range. If the source, such as an electronic document, does not have numbered pages, follow the APA's rules to include the paragraph number if the paragraph numbers are visible. If neither page numbers nor paragraph numbers are visible, then cite the heading if it is available, and the number of the paragraph in the section in which the material is located (APA, 2010, p. 172). If the headings are lengthy, you can use a shortened title enclosed in quotation marks. If no publication year is indicated, use the abbreviation n.d. without extra spacing to indicate "no date." The in-text citation would be either Author (n.d.) or in parentheses (Author, n.d.).

Reference list entries should be in alphabetical order. As mentioned above, you should use surnames only for in-text citations, and the date of publication if it is available. If there is no date shown, then use the abbreviation n.d. for "no date," and remember that there should be no spaces added to internal abbreviations like n.d. and U.S. If the author is unnamed and you have elevated the title of the work to the author position, alphabetize the entry in the reference list by using the first significant word of the title.

With Word 2007, Microsoft introduced a powerful feature for managing sources and adding both in-text citations and reference list entries. This feature was continued in Word 2010, which as a bonus provides APA 6th edition formatting as one of the style choices. However, you will find that the reference tool is only as good as the knowledge of the person using it, and if you do not know how to use it properly, it will not produce APA-compliant formatting. In Chapter 5, I demonstrate how to use the bibliographic tools in Word for both in-text citations and reference lists.

As I mentioned previously, there are many software programs that purport to produce APA style, but in my experience, every one of them results in incorrect format. You will also find that databases like ProQuest provide "APA" citations, but they are usually, if not always, incorrect in one or more ways. You will find that most universities have writing centers, many of which provide presentations and instructions, along with sample papers. Although these are helpful, you may find that not all their instructions result in correct APA style. When in doubt, consult the APA manual or the APA style web site and blog.

Formatting Citations and References to Books and Articles

In the body of your text, the titles of books and journals should be italicized. They should be in title case, as discussed above. In the reference list, journal titles should still be in title case and italics, but book titles should not be in title case, though they should still be in italics. The inclusion of a book, journal, or article title in the text rarely adds value to your paper, because the title will also appear in the reference list. Instead, use APA's preferred author-date form of citation in your text. Look at the formatting examples of the various books in the example reference list at the end of the Chapter 3. The first word of the title is always capitalized, but other words should not be capitalized unless they are proper nouns or are the first word after a colon or a dash in the title. For example, in the text of your document, should you desire to give the full title of the APA manual, you would use the following title:

Publication Manual of the American Psychological Association (6th ed.).

However, in the reference list, the word "manual" should not be capitalized because it is not a proper noun. The words "Publication" and "American Psychological Association" should be capitalized because Publication is the first word, and because American Psychological Association is a proper noun. Here is how the reference should be formatted in your reference list. Note that there is no punctuation between the title and the parenthetical edition information, and that the edition information and parentheses are not to be italicized. See also that the "th" following 6 is not superscripted. I show you below how to accomplish this.

American Psychological Association. (2010*). Publication manual of the American Psychological Association* (6th ed.). Washington, DC: Author.

When the author is also the publisher, as is true in this case, the word "Author" is used to designate the publisher. Because APA is a well-known abbreviation, you can cite the APA manual in your text as I have done previously in this book, using the format APA (2010) or in parentheses (APA, 2010).

As I mentioned, references in APA style do not superscript the "th" after 6, but Word does this automatically by default. If you type 6 and then "th" without spacing, you will get 6th. However, you can easily fix this in either of two simple ways. You can simply insert a space after 6 and then type "th," and then remove the space. You will be left with "6th." Another thing you can do is to use the little superscript icon in the Font group on the Home ribbon. Selecting the "th" and then clicking on the $\times^2$ icon will "un-superscript" the "th." You can also use a keyboard shortcut to do this, by holding down <**Ctrl**> + <**Shift**> and then pressing the + key. This works like a toggle switch, turning on and then turning off the superscripting. The icon immediately to the left of this one works the same way when you need to type something with a subscript or to remove a subscript (see Figure 35).

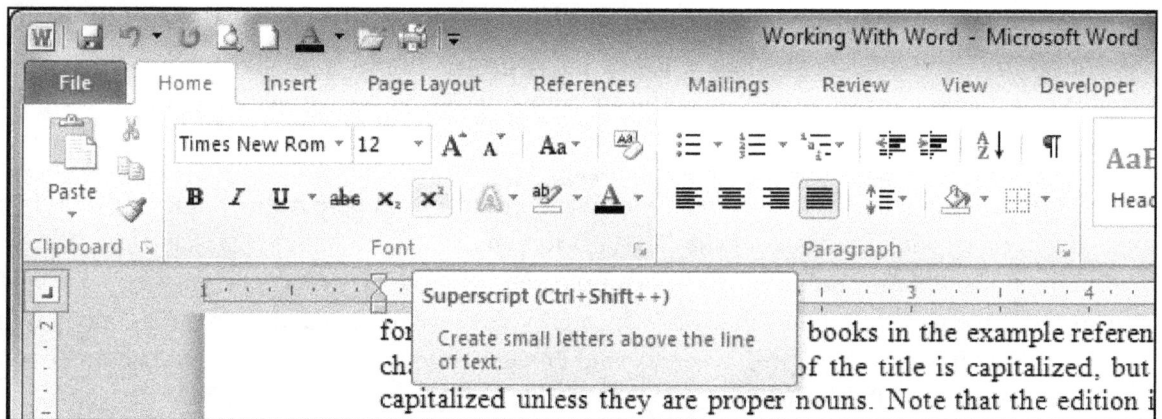

Figure 35. Use this icon to superscript or to "unsuperscript."

When the author of a book is named, you should use the following general format for your reference list entry.

Author, A. A. (Year). *Title of book.* City, ST: Publisher.

In the text, you would refer to this work as Author (Year), or in parentheses (Author, Year).

If there are two authors, you should cite both authors each time you refer to the source. The general format is:

Author, A. A., & Author, B. B. (Year). *Title of book*. City, ST: Publisher.

You should insert a space between authors' initials, and there should be a comma after the initials of the first author in the reference list, even when there are only two authors. In the text, you would refer to this work as Firstauthor and Secondauthor (Year), or in parentheses as (Firstauthor & Secondauthor, Year). If a work has three to five authors, list all authors the first time you refer to the work. For every subsequent citation of the same work, you should cite only the surname of the first author followed by no comma and et al. followed by a comma and the year. Here is a reference to one of my favorite business statistics textbooks:

Lind, D. A., Marchal, W. G., & Wathen, S. A. (2010). *Statistical techniques in business & economics* (14th ed.). Boston, MA: McGraw-Hill Irwin.

In the text, refer to this work the first time you cite it as Lind, Marchal, and Wathen (2010), or in parentheses as (Lind, Marchal, & Wathen, 2010). You should use & for parenthetical citations and reference list entries, but you should spell out and in the body of the document. For any subsequent citations of this book, use Lind et al. (2010) in the text and (Lind et al., 2010) in parentheses. Even for well-known cities like Boston and New York, the two-letter state abbreviation is now required by APA. If the book was not published in the U.S., you should include both the city and the country, as in London, England or Manila, Republic of the Philippines (APA, 2010, p. 187).

When a work has six or more authors, you should cite only the first author's name for the first and all subsequent citations of that work in the text of your document, as in Pace et al. (2010) or in parentheses (Pace et al., 2010). In the reference list, when a source has six or seven authors, list all authors' names in the reference list, using the general format shown above. According to the APA manual (APA, 2010, p. 199), "When a reference has up to seven authors, spell out all authors' names in the reference list."

Occasionally, you might cite a reference with eight or more authors. In that unusual event, APA says to use the following format (APA, 2010, p. 198). This is the example from the APA manual. Use ellipsis points (…) to separate the names of the first six authors from the name of the last author listed. The digital object identifier (DOI) should be used in preference to any other form of citation or retrieval information if a DOI has been assigned to the article. Like a reference ending with a web address (URL), citations ending with a DOI should not be followed by a period. APA says not to capitalize DOI in the reference list. Do not insert any spacing after the colon in the DOI.

Gilbert, D. G., McClernon, J. F., Rabinovich, N. E., Sugai, C., Plath, L. C., Asgaard, G., … Botros, N. (2004). Effects of quitting smoking on EEG activation and attention last for more than 31 days and are more severe with stress, dependence, DRD2 A1 allele, and depressive traits. *Nicotine and Tobacco Research, 6*, 249-267. doi:10.1080/1462220041001676306

Every citation of this source in the text should be Gilbert et al. (2004), or in parentheses (Gilbert et al., 2004). Note there should be no comma before et al. The APA style blog gives an example of a source with a whopping 187 authors! As with the example above, only the first six authors and the last author should be named in the reference list.

More on Formatting References to Journal Articles

As the last citation above shows, you should italicize both the title of the journal and the volume number. The titles of the articles themselves vary depending on their location in the document. In a parenthetical citation, you should type the first few words of the title of the article in title case and enclose it in quotation marks. However, in the reference list, you should not use title case or quotation marks unless they are part of the title itself.

The general format for a periodical such as a journal, magazine, newspaper, or newsletter article is as follows (APA, 2010, p. 198):

Author, A. A., Author B. B., & Author, C. C. (Year). Title of article. *Title of Periodical*, xx, pp-pp.
doi:xx.xxxxxxxxx

When you are citing a newspaper article, follow the year with the month and the day.

With a DOI, as I mentioned above, the general rule to include a space after a colon should not be followed, and there should be no space between the letters doi, the colon, and the actual DOI. If you retrieved a source online, APA says to include the DOI if one is assigned to the document. If you located the article through a database like ProQuest, you can look in the indexing information to determine whether there is a DOI or not. You can also use the free DOI lookup tool provided by CrossRef at the following web address:

http://www.crossref.org/guestquery/

If you cannot locate a DOI, the APA manual says to determine if you can find the article through a publicly available web site. If so, you should cite that in preference to the database information. For more information on DOIs and URLs, APA has provided a flowchart to show you what to do in various situations. You do not need to include the DOI if you are citing the print version of an article. Here is a link:

http://blog.apastyle.org/files/doi-and-url-flowchart-8.pdf

As a last resort, if there is no DOI and there is no publicly available web access to the article, you should cite either the database retrieval information and the document ID or accession number, or the actual URL from which you retrieved the document. This is one area where APA gives you a choice in the matter. According to the APA manual:

In general, it is not necessary to include database information. Journal coverage in a particular database may change over time; also, if using an aggregator such as EBSCO, OVID, or ProQuest (each of which contain many discipline-specific databases, such as PsycINFO), it may be unclear exactly which database provided the full text of an article. (APA, 2010, p. 192)

These instructions conflict with the "APA" citations suggested by ProQuest and other database aggregators. With the newest APA manual, users are instructed not to include the retrieval date except in rare circumstances such as a citation of a wiki or a blog that is updated over time or a source that is in limited circulation. Otherwise, APA says rather flatly to omit the retrieval date (APA, 2010, p. 192).

Frequently, the database will show all caps for article titles, "Anonymous" for the author, and two periods in a row as in Author, A. A.. (Year). These are all erroneous in APA reference list entries. The two periods result from a computer scripting error. You should never cite "Anonymous" as the author of a work unless the work is actually signed "By Anonymous." You should not use n.a. for no author, nor should you use "Unknown." Often a corporate author, such as APA or General Motors, is easy to identify. Otherwise, when a work is produced by an unknown author, elevate the title of the work to the author position. In the reference list, your entry would now be:

Title of work goes here not in title case. (Year). *Title of Periodical in Italics and Title Case if Known*. Retrieved from http://www.webaddress.com

The retrieval date is not included. Do not put a period after the web address. There should be no colon after from. See that the title of the work is not in italics. In the text, refer to this source in title case and quotes, as in "Title of Work" (Year), or in parentheses as ("Title of Work," Year). Here is the APA manual's own example of a citation of a newsletter article retrieved from the web (APA, 2010, p. 200). Remember there is no period after the URL because it would appear to be part of the web address, as periods are used to separate parts of the URL.

Six sites meet for comprehensive anti-gang initiative conference. (2006, November/December). *OJJDP News @ a Glance*. Retrieved from http:www.ncjrs.gov/html/ojjdpnews_at_glance/216684/topstory.html

The exact URL is helpful here. There is no retrieval date, and you would refer to this source in the text as "Six Sites Meet" (2006), or in parentheses as ("Six Sites Meet," 2006). As APA style requires, the comma following Meet in the parenthetical citation goes INSIDE the quotation marks, not after them.

Many journal articles show both volume and issue numbers. You must always provide the volume number. The issue number is required only for journals that start the page numbering with page 1 for each issue. Otherwise, you should not provide the issue number. The issue number, when it is needed, should be in parentheses immediately after the volume number. The volume number should be italicized, but the parentheses and the issue number should not be. Do not use p. or pp. before the page number(s) in journal citations, though you should use p. or pp. for page or pages for citations of newspaper articles (APA, 2010, p. 200).

Databases Get the Format Wrong

Let us take a short side trip to an online library where we will find and correctly cite a journal article, and you will see what is wrong with pasting the "Cite this" information into your document, even when ProQuest and other databases tell you to do exactly that. You will usually find the Advanced Search features of a library database to be more helpful than the Basic Search. I typically limit my search to full text documents and scholarly peer-reviewed journals. Peer review is the gold standard for research, and such journal articles are usually considered more credible than information you retrieve by using Google or some other search engine. Because I am personally interested in statistics education, I searched for articles with those two keywords. I got over 10,000 hits because these are popular words in article citations and abstracts. However, when I accepted ProQuest's reasonable suggestion to combine the search terms, and limited my search to full-text article in scholarly journals, I got a more manageable list of 184 articles. One of the studies I located analyzed the use of student self-grading in a statistics class.

Here is what ProQuest gave me (Figure 36). When I looked at the indexing information, there was no DOI listed, but the CrossRef lookup tool discussed above easily located the DOI for this article. When you have the DOI, you should NOT cite the database retrieval information or a web site. You should also not include the retrieval date, as discussed above. The title of the article appears in all caps in the database. This is not correct format, though many students simply paste the information directly into their reference lists.

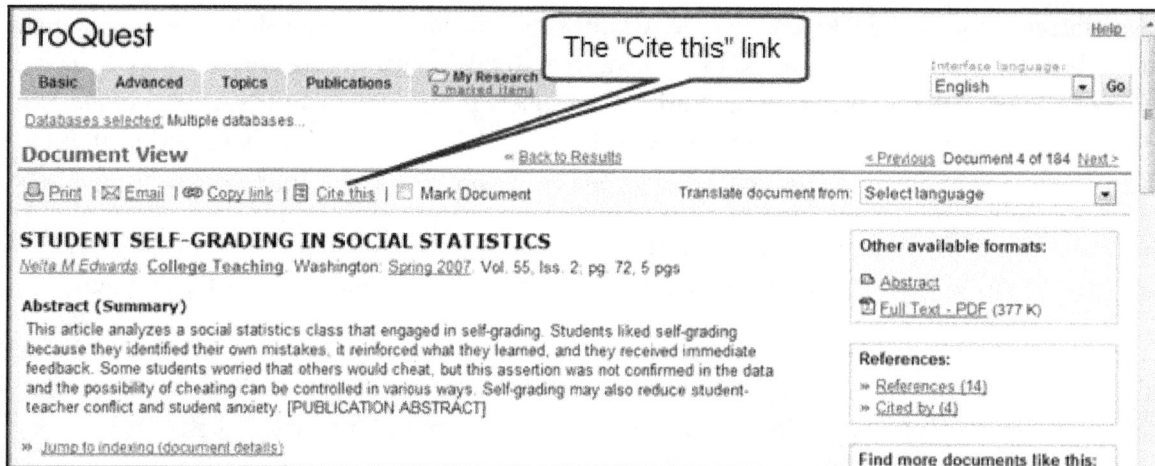

Figure 36. Finding the "Cite this" link in ProQuest

You can get something approximating APA style by clicking on the Cite this link from the Document View (see Figure 36). Here is what you get (Figure 37).

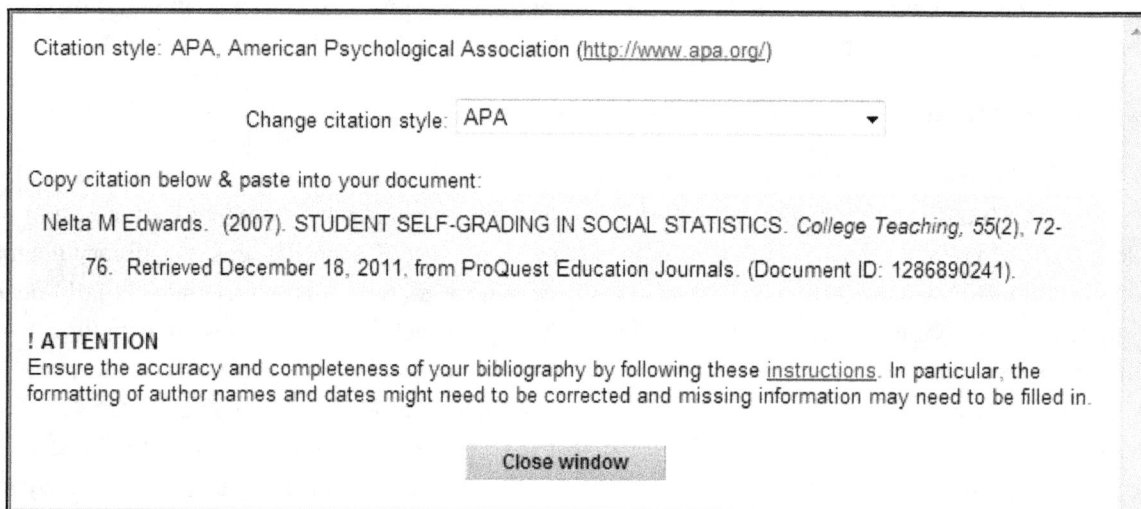

Figure 37. ProQuest's suggested "APA" citation

Some students stop there, and follow the instructions to copy and paste the citation into their documents, perhaps not even changing the font or the indentation. Although this is better than the original information, it is still far from correct. Note the following errors in the citation. In APA style, references are entered with the author's surname, followed by initials. First and middle names are NOT spelled out. Each initial should have a period after it. Titles of articles in the reference list should not be in all caps or in title case. The retrieval date is no longer routinely used, and because there is a DOI, it should be cited instead of the ProQuest Document ID. One thing ProQuest does get right is the italics for the journal title and the volume number. Here is the correct citation, as it should appear in your reference list:

Edwards, N. M. (2007). Student self-grading in social statistics. *College Teaching, 55*(2), 72-76. doi:10.3200/CTCH.55.2.72-76

To cite this article in the text of your document, use Edwards (2007) or, in parentheses, (Edwards, 2007).

Citing Information You Find on the Internet

The Internet is the source of a wealth of information, but there is also a great deal of biased material and misinformation on the Internet. Before you cite a source you find on the Internet, you should verify its credibility. Many university libraries provide guidelines for evaluating web-based sources. One very good one is that of Cornell University:

http://olinuris.library.cornell.edu/ref/research/webeval.html

If you verify the credibility of the information you found on the Internet and refer to this information in your paper, you should cite it. The APA manual gives some general guidelines, and the APA Style blog provides very helpful detail and examples. Here is a link:

http://blog.apastyle.org/apastyle/2010/11/how-to-cite-something-you-found-on-a-website-in-apa-style.html

If you are citing an entire web site, you should not include the link to the site in the reference list but put it in your text only. For example, you might want to communicate that the APA style blog (http://blog.apastyle.org/) is a useful site. However, when you cite or quote information on a specific web page, you should give the web address (URL) in your reference list. Often, the author is unidentified, but the corporate author is easy to identify, and you should use the corporate author in the author position. For example, you might want to cite specific information at the site mentioned above in the following way:

The APA style blog instructs users not to italicize the names of documents or web pages (Lee, 2010).

In the reference list, you refer to this source in the following way. The APA manual instructs us to include the retrieval date here because the contents of blogs may change over time.

Lee, C. (2010, November 18). How to cite something you found on a website in APA style [Web log post]. Retrieved July 2, 2012 from http://blog.apastyle.org/apastyle/2010/11/how-to-cite-something-you-found-on-a-website-in-apa-style.html

The reference list entry would be alphabetized by author's name, just as you would alphabetize any other entry. As discussed above, if the author or corporate author cannot be identified, you would promote the title to the author position in the reference list entry and use an in-text citation with the first few words of the title in title case and enclosed in quotation marks. Use enough of the title to specify the work clearly.

APA's general rule for citing information you locate on the Internet is as follows (adapted from Lee, 2010):

Author, A. (date). Title of document or web page [Format description]. Retrieved from http://www.webaddress.com

See that the title of the document or web page should NOT be italicized. The format description is necessary only when the material is something out of the ordinary such as a blog post, lecture notes, or an electronic document such as a Nook or Kindle eBook. Although many of the formatting examples in various university writing centers show the titles of web pages in italics, you should follow the APA rules here. In addition to the above information, APA also makes available a table in which you can find what you should do when required parts of a citation are missing.

http://blog.apastyle.org/files/how-to-cite-something-you-found-on-a-website-in-apa-style---table-1.pdf

Looking Ahead

Now that you know how to get the references right, let us look in Chapter 5 at using the built-in bibliographic tools of Word.

Chapter 5—Using the Bibliography Tools

Word's bibliography tools are very helpful for several reasons. One major reason is that you can build a master list of sources for your research papers and reuse these sources in different papers. Another is that you can insert in-text citations. I do not usually find this helpful, but I will illustrate it for you, just in case you might like to use it. One of the best reasons to use these tools is that you can insert a reference list, and if you have set the default normal font to 12-point Times New Roman and the default line spacing to double spacing, you can get the formatting perfect (or very nearly so) every time. This, of course, depends on how well you know APA format, and how effectively you use the bibliographic tools.

Adding a Reference to an Article

Let us use the bibliographic tools to enter the information about the Edwards (2007) article we found earlier. Although you can get everything right, you still have to put the information in the right fields of the database, which is what you are actually creating. These references will be available to you with any new document you create from the same computer, making the tool very useful for research papers, theses, and dissertations. If there is a reference, like that to a current textbook, that you cite regularly, consider adding it to your sources.

Here is how to enter the information for a journal article. Click on the References tab and locate the Citations & Bibliography group. With Word 2010, you can choose APA Sixth Edition as your formatting style (Figure 38). You still have to know APA format here, but this tool makes it easy to put everything where it needs to be if you know how to find the right places.

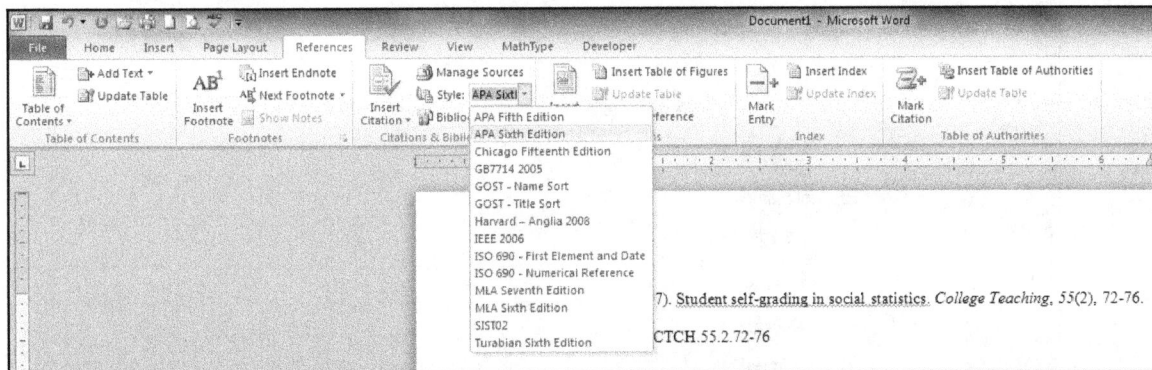

Figure 38. Using the Citations & Bibliography group

To add a new source, click on Manage Sources. The Source Manager will open, and you must click on New to add the new source (See Figure 39).

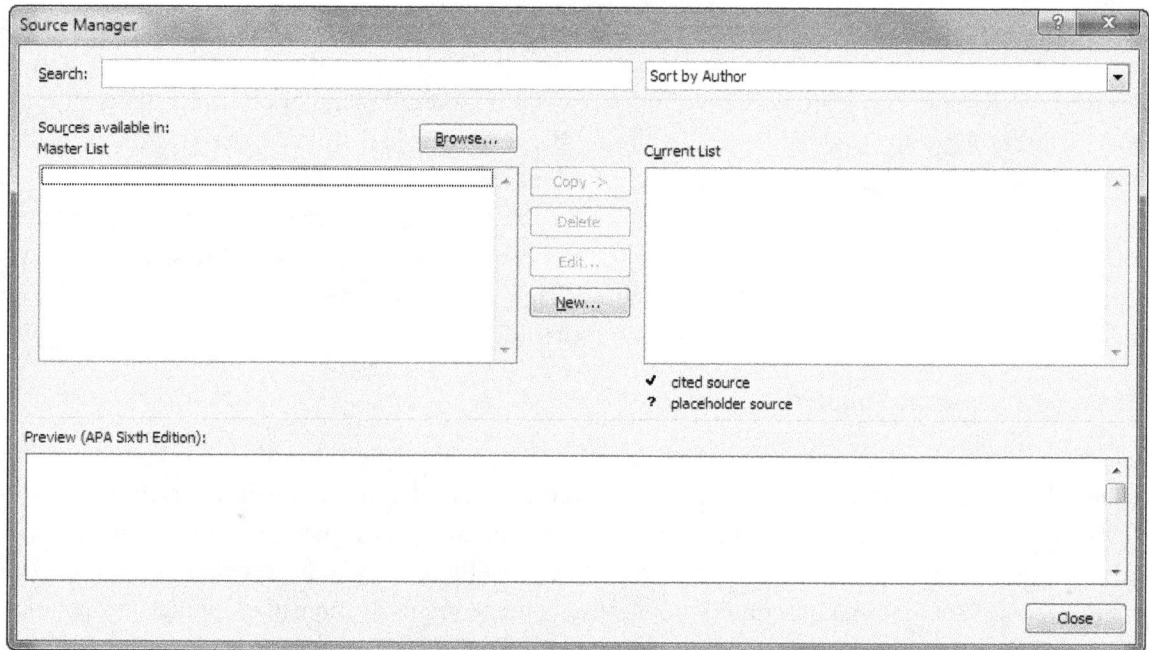

Figure 39. The Source Manager dialog box. Click on "New" to create a new reference.

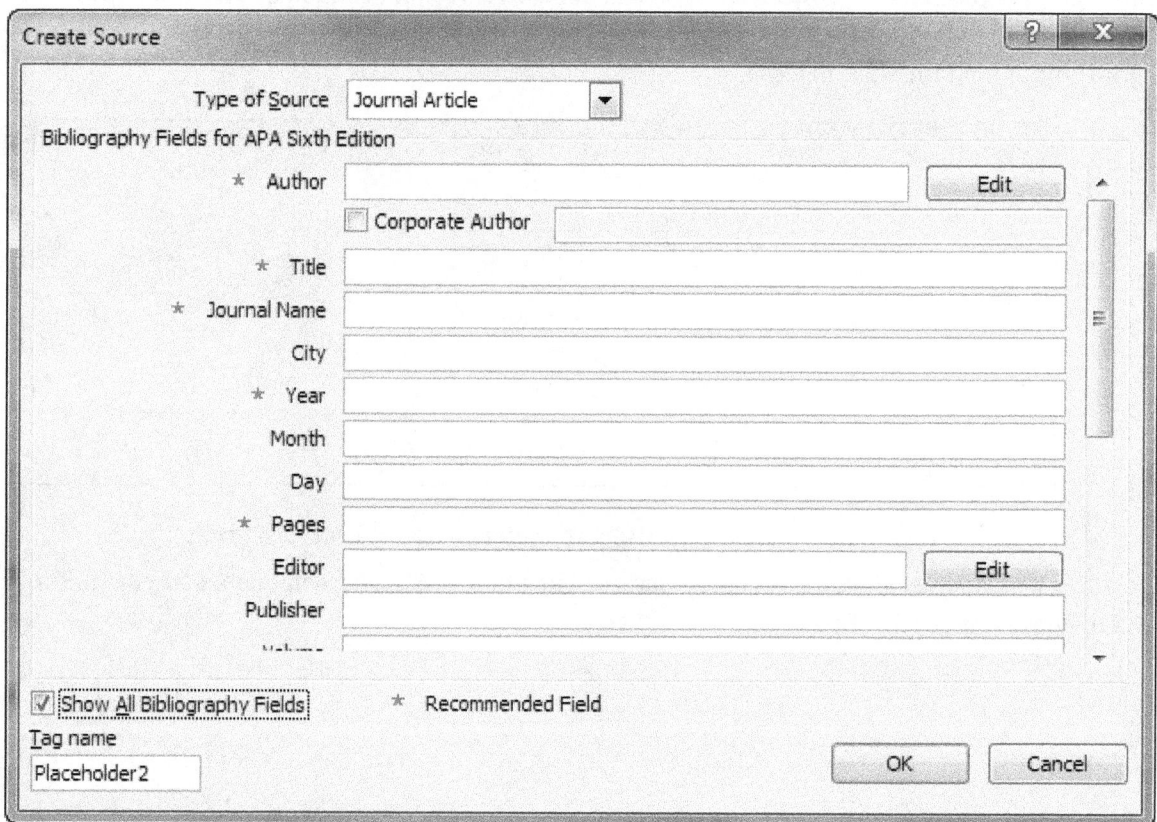

Figure 40. The Create Source dialog. Make sure to select "Show All Bibliography Fields."

Make sure the type of source you select is Journal Article. When you click on Create Source, or when you edit the information, you should always click on Show All Bibliography Fields (see Figure 40).

Click on Edit to enter the author information. You can just use initials if you like, because APA style does not use first names in the reference list. Even if you put the author's name in the field, the bibliographic tools will provide the initial rather than the name in the reference list if you have selected APA Sixth Edition as your style choice.

Type the title and other information as shown below (see Figure 41). You will have to scroll down to find the correct fields for the volume, issue, and DOI entries (Figure 42). Even though these are not marked as recommended fields, they are needed to get the format exactly right.

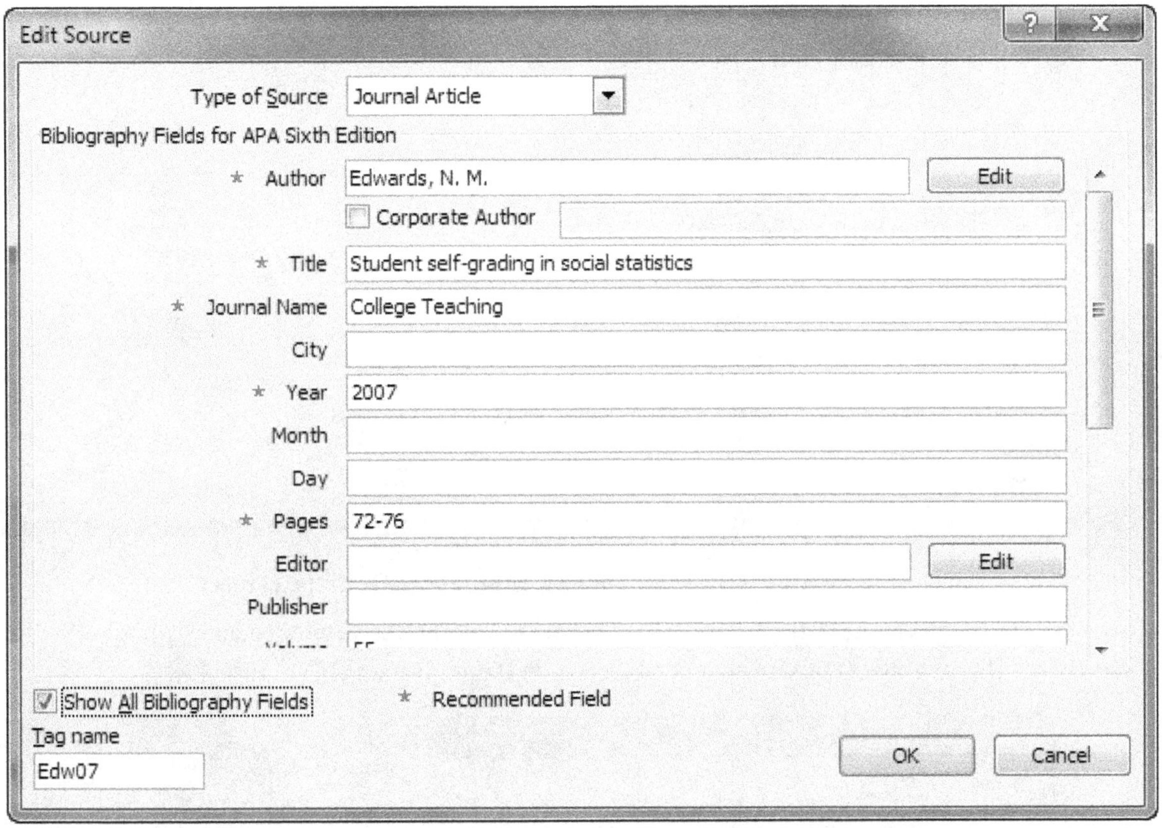

Figure 41. Entering information for a journal article

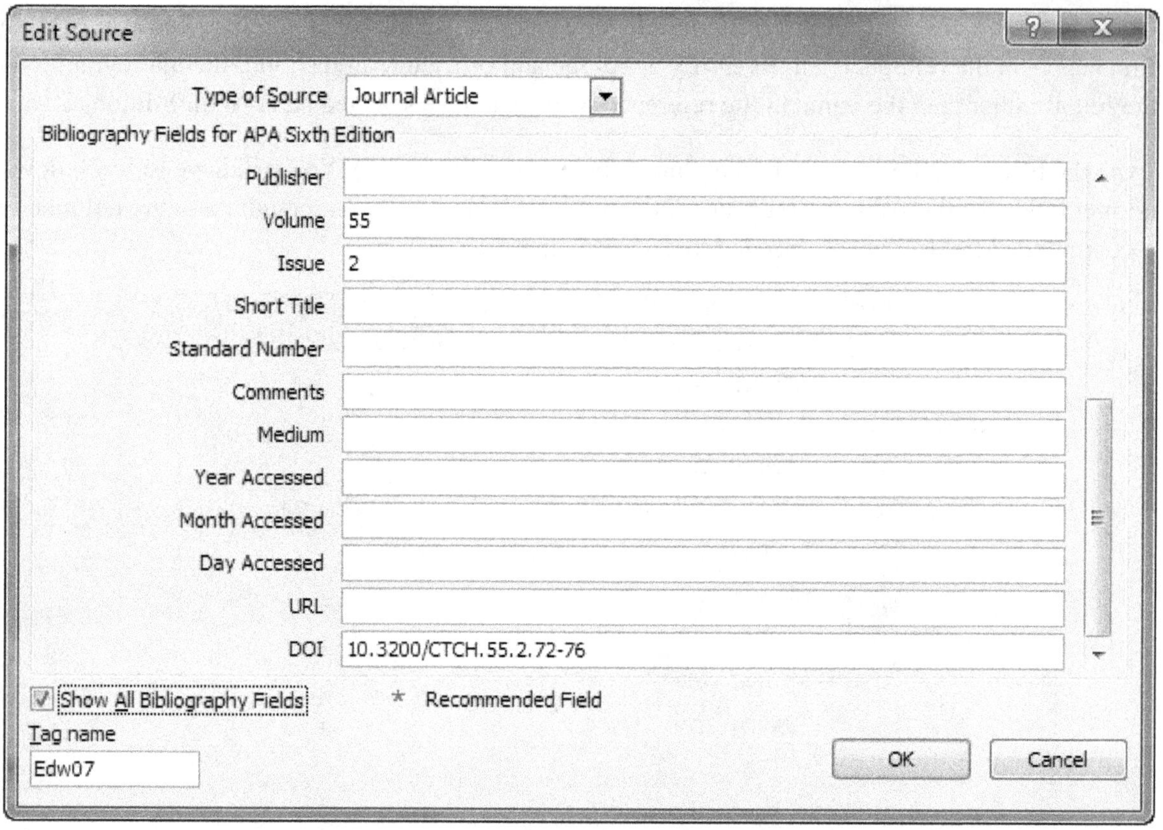

Figure 42. Put the volume, issue, and DOI in the correct fields

Now, see that when you have the information entered correctly, the reference entry preview will be formatted correctly too, though it will obviously not be shown in the required font (Figure 43).

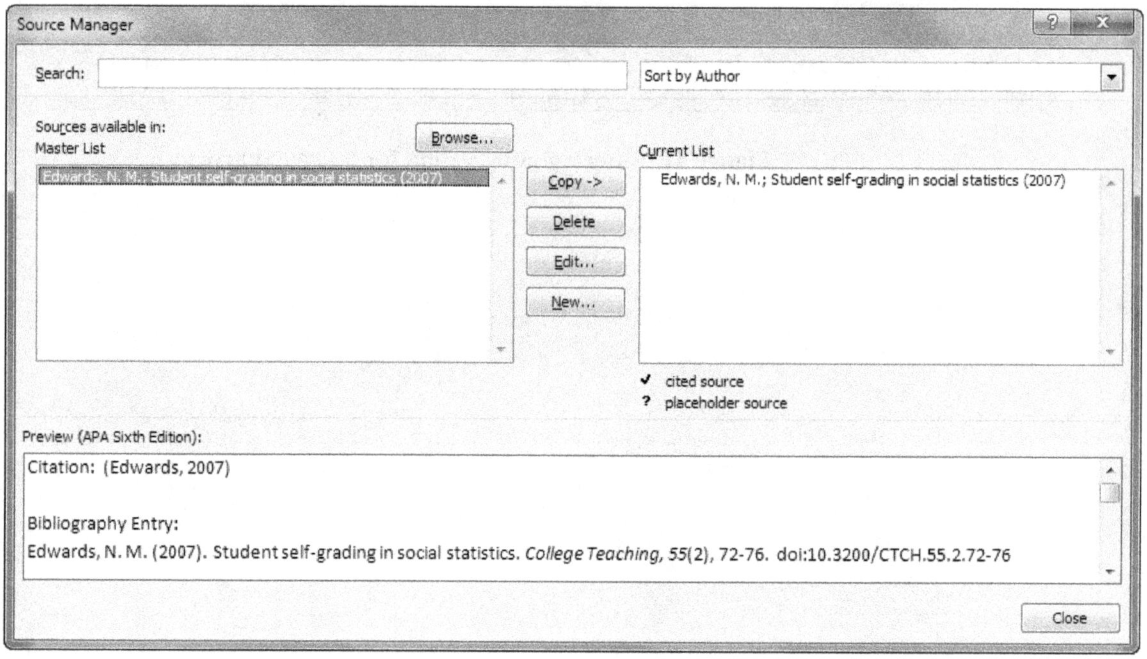

Figure 43. Notice the preview of the correctly formatted reference list entry

See that the source is now available in the Master List and in the Current List (the document you are editing). If you use the tool to insert a citation, the reference will be identified as "cited," and you will not be able to delete the reference from your document unless you remove the citation.

Adding a Reference to a Book

Let us add the reference to the APA manual next. As we discussed, the manual is a book with a corporate author, and the author is the publisher. Click on Manage Sources again, select New, and set the type to Book. As with the journal article, enter the information in the correct fields. Remember you need to enter the two-letter state (or district in this case) abbreviation. You will have to scroll down to find the field for the edition. Enter 6th (as discussed above) here. As the screens are very similar to those for journal articles, I do not show all the screen captures, but I do show you the preview below (Figure 44).

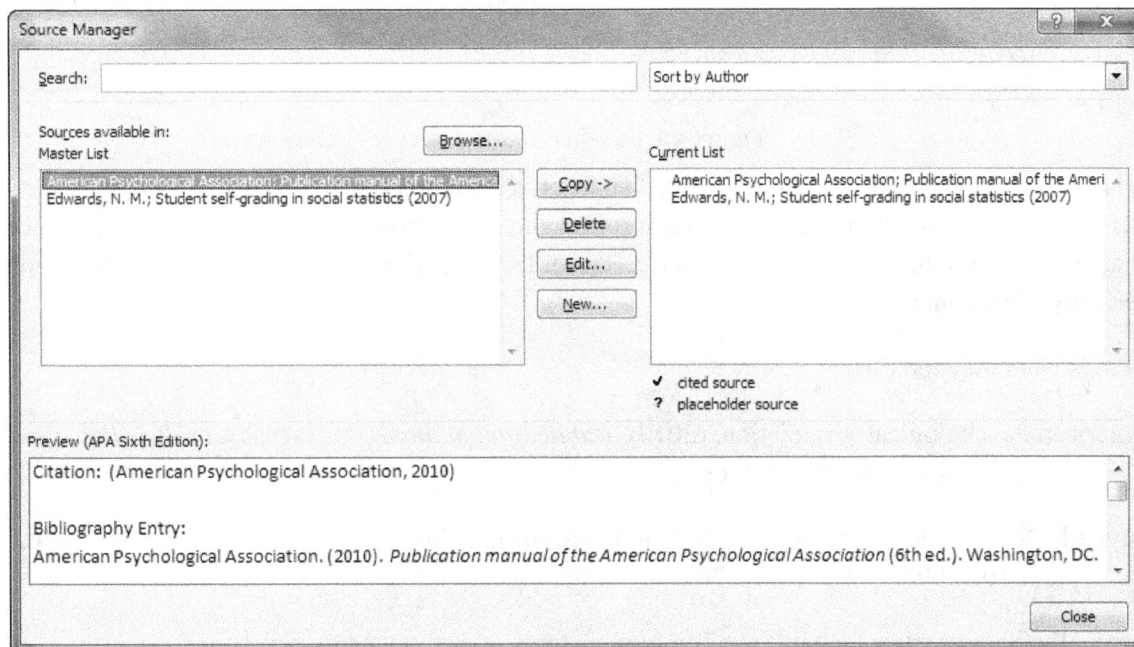

Figure 44. Adding the reference to the APA manual

Inserting the Reference List

Remember the word "manual" should not be capitalized in the reference list. Now, here is how to insert your reference list. Although there are links to insert a Bibliography or a Works Cited list, you should avoid those, and instead click on the link at the bottom (see Figure 45) to get the reference list in a better format.

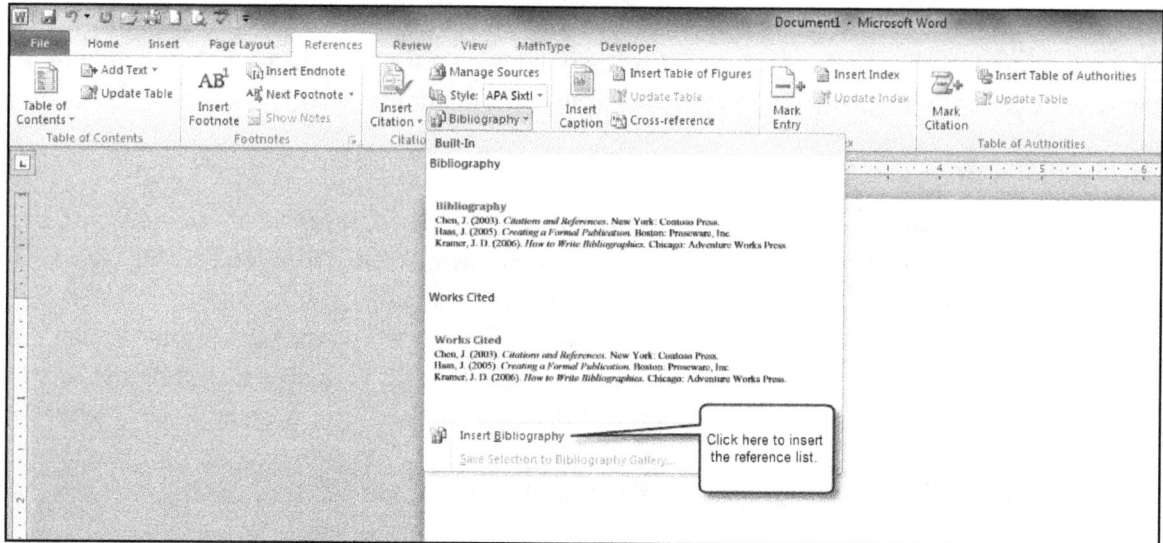

Figure 45. Use this icon to insert the reference list.

When you are ready to insert the reference list, insert a page break (**<Ctrl>** + **<Enter>**), and then center the word References at the top of the new page. Then follow the instructions above to insert your references. Because we entered them into the Source Manager in the correct format and used the correct fields, the references will be perfectly APA compliant.

Here is what they look like:

American Psychological Association. (2010). *Publication manual of the American Psychological Association* (6th ed.). Washington, DC: Author.

Edwards, N. M. (2007). Student self-grading in social statistics. *College Teaching, 55*(2), 72-76. doi:10.3200/CTCH.55.2.72-76

Again, the biggest advantage of the bibliographic tools is that you can store the references in your master list and use them whenever needed. This is very helpful for literature reviews, research papers, and especially theses and dissertations.

Inserting In-text Citations

The bibliographic tools also allow us to insert in-text citations, and to customize them as necessary. As I mentioned, if you use this feature, the reference will be linked to your document, and you cannot delete it unless you delete the citation as well. When you enter the citation, you can also convert it to static text, which will be very helpful for your instructor or classmates when they are working on editing or peer reviewing your paper, as it is not possible to edit the citation easily because it is actually a field in your document. Your instructor cannot comment on it, either. Assuming you have already identified APA as the abbreviation for the American Psychological Association, you can just use APA. Here is the Insert Citation command (Figure 46).

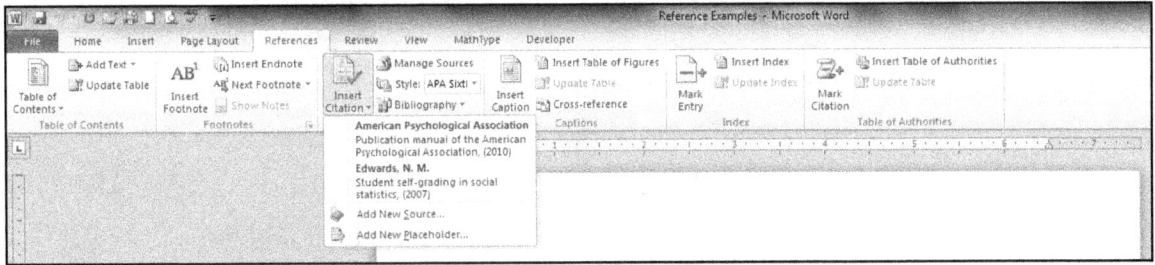

Figure 46. Inserting an in-text citation

When we click on the APA manual citation, this is what is what we will get:

(American Psychological Association, 2010)

This is fine for most references, but because APA is a well-known abbreviation, we can click on the reference and delete the author information. When you click on the citation, you have a dropdown menu available to you (see Figure 47). Just select Edit Citation. You can add a page or page range if you need to (for example when you make a direct quote), and can suppress the other information as desired. Then, convert the citation to static text and add APA in front of the year. This is so much work it is probably easier just to type (APA, 2010), but many students like using the bibliographic tools to insert their citations, so now you know how to do it, too.

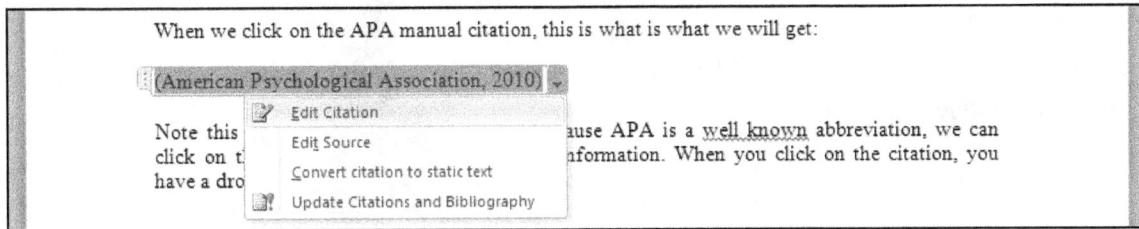

Figure 47. Editing an in-text citation

Here is the edited reference.

(APA, 2010)

Because we cited it, the reference to the APA manual is now a "cited" source and will have a check mark in front of it in the Current List. You will not be able to delete the reference from the Current List at this point, as the "Delete" button is grayed out in the dialog when you click on the reference in the Current List.

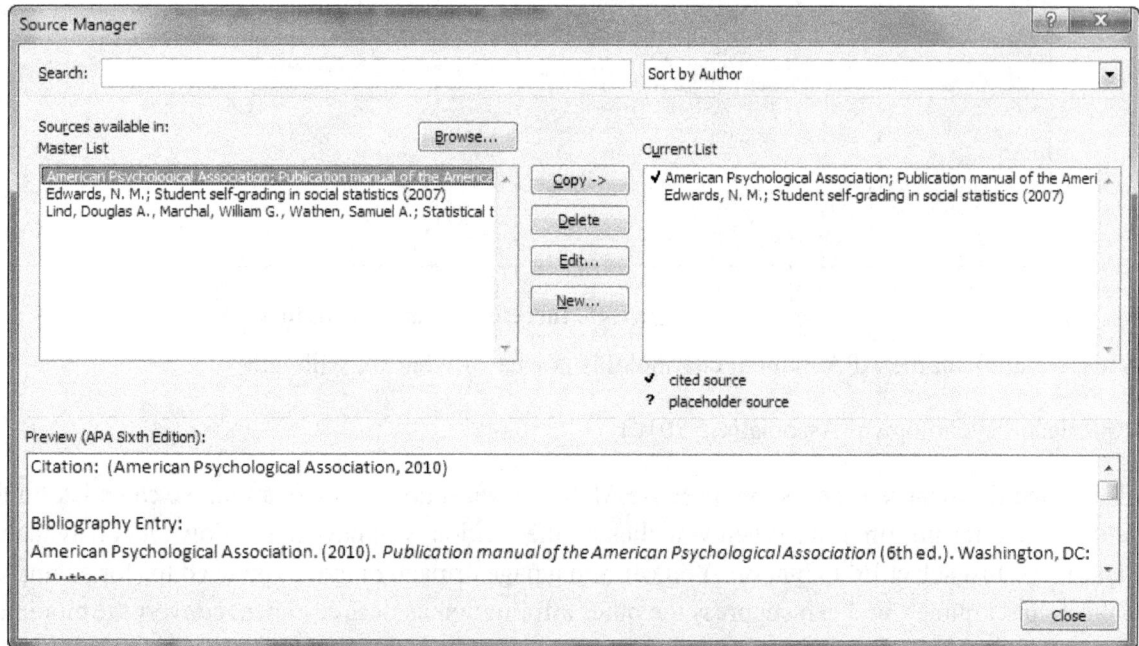

Figure 48. Notice the check mark next to a cited source

Looking Ahead

In Chapter 6, I address another problematic issue, namely that of reporting and formatting statistical results in correct APA style.

Chapter 6—Formatting Statistics in APA Style

Because I teach statistics and research methods courses in addition to conducting various research studies, I have had to learn the fine points of APA style concerning the formatting of statistics and statistical results. Just as the formatting standards for text have changed over the years, so have those for statistics and mathematical copy. Although these are covered in the APA manual, the instructions are difficult to understand and are located in different places in the manual. The APA manual assumes a level of statistical sophistication most student writers do not possess. Thus, the formatting of statistics and statistical results is a particularly troublesome area for most students, who are often learning statistics at the same time they are being required to learn and use APA format.

Statisticians in a variety of fields are frankly unconcerned with APA style, but researchers and students in psychology, education, and many other behavioral and social sciences are frequently required to follow the instructions in the APA manual. Many universities have simply adopted APA style as their universal standard for all disciplines. All APA journals, obviously, and many other journals, including those of the American Psychological Society, require APA style. If you are required to use APA format, APA's standards for formatting statistics and statistical results also apply to your student papers, theses, and dissertations.

In this chapter, I explain the APA rules for formatting statistics and statistical results. I cover the number of decimals to report, the correct way to format APA-style summary statements and tables containing statistical information and what to include when you report statistical results.

Statistics and Parameters

We use statistics to make inferences about populations from the data in samples. The population is the entire collection of objects or individuals of interest. A sample is a subset of a population. A measurable characteristic of a population is called a parameter, while a measurable characteristic of a sample is called a statistic. Although there are a few exceptions, Latin letters (what you can think of as the normal English alphabet) are generally used to represent sample statistics, while Greek letters are used to represent population parameters. APA says that the letters used to represent statistics should be displayed in italics. Examples include t, F, N, n, p, r, and z. These should not be in boldface unless the letter happens to represent a matrix or vector.

As indicated above, population parameters and some sample statistics are generally represented by Greek letters. APA says these should not be italicized, though they frequently are shown italicized in statistics books. Examples of correct APA format include μ, β, χ^2, η^2, and λ. Most of these characters can be found by using the **Insert** > **Symbols** > **Symbol** dialog. Click on More Symbols. Scroll down to find the Greek and Coptic characters. Occasionally, you will need to use both a superscript and a subscript, and when this is necessary, you cannot do both simultaneously using Word's basic features. Instead, you can click on **Insert** > **Symbols** > **Equation** to launch the built-in equation editor. Click Insert New Equation. When you do this, you will now have access to the Equation Tools with a Design tab and various formatting options (see Figure 49). If you simply click on the word Equation or the Greek pi icon, you will automatically insert a box for a new equation, and the Equation Tools will open.

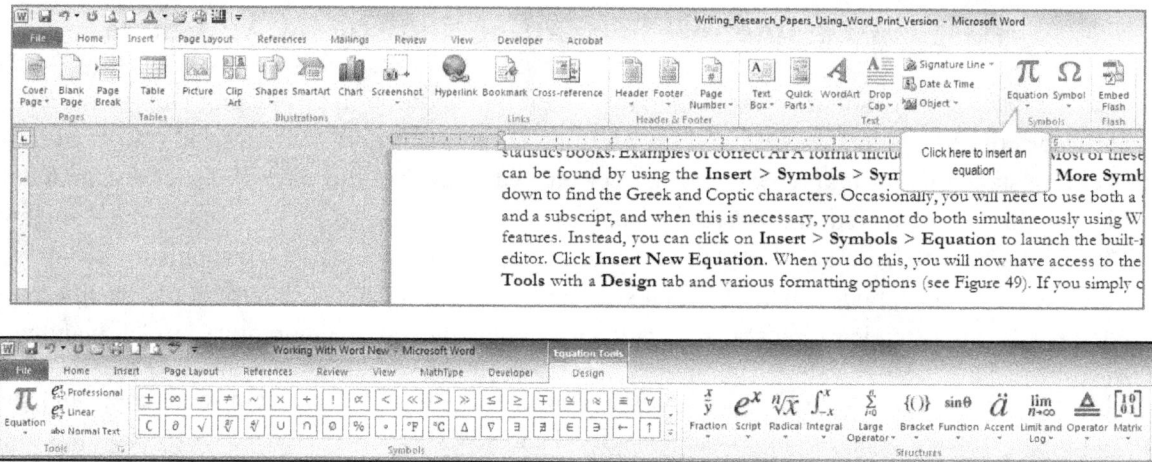

Figure 49. The Equation Tools

Assume for example that you have conducted a complex analysis of variance and need to report an effect size index known as "partial eta squared." Here is what it should look like:

$$\eta_p^2$$

To insert the eta with both a subscripted p and a superscripted 2, click on the icon labeled Script. Find the symbols that show a box followed by both subscript and superscript boxes. Word will insert an "inline" equation by default, which will appear as part of your document text. Now, just click in the boxes and type in the η, the p, and the 2. Word will automatically format the eta in italics, but you should click on it and change it to regular text.

Symbols and Abbreviations

When you use statistical terms in the body of your text, you should write them out, for example standard deviation, median, mean, and range (APA, 2010, p. 117). Certain statistical terms are typically abbreviated in both the text and in tables, such as *df* for degrees of freedom, *n* for sample size or *N* for population size, *r* for a correlation coefficient, and *p* for probability. In tables and parentheses, you should use the APA manual's list of acceptable symbols and abbreviations (APA, 2010, pp. 119-123). Abbreviations commonly used in tables and parentheses include *M* for mean and *SD* for standard deviation. Here is a summary of some of the symbols and abbreviations commonly used in reporting statistics and statistical results (Table 1). As referenced above, the APA manual provides a more extensive table.

Table 1. APA-approved symbols and abbreviations for statistical terms

Symbol or Abbreviation	How to Say It	Interpretation
ANOVA		Analysis of variance
CI		Confidence interval
df		Degrees of freedom
F		Fisher's F statistic
M or $\bar{X}$	M or "X-bar"	Mean (use M in tables or parentheses, otherwise spell out mean).
MANOVA		Multivariate analysis of variance
n		Sample size, group size
N		Entire sample size, population size
p		Probability, proportion
R		Multiple correlation coefficient
r		Correlation coefficient
s	Standard deviation	Sample standard deviation
s^2	Variance	Sample variance
SD		Standard deviation (use SD in tables or parentheses, otherwise spell out standard deviation).
t		Gosett's t statistic
T		Test statistic for Wilcoxon signed-ranks test
U		Test statistic for Mann-Whitney test
$\hat{y}$	"y-hat"	Predicted value of y in regression
z		z score
α	Alpha	Alpha level, probability of Type I error
β	Beta	Beta level, probability of Type II error, Standardized regression coefficient
μ	Mu (pronounced "mew")	Population mean
η^2	Eta squared	Eta squared (effect-size index)
φ	Phi (statisticians typically pronounce this as "fee," not "figh")	Phi coefficient (effect-size index for chi-square tests)
ρ	Rho (pronounced "row")	Population correlation coefficient
σ	Sigma	Population standard deviation
Σ	Sigma or "sum of"	Summation operator
σ^2	Sigma squared	Population variance
χ^2	Chi square (pronounced "kigh square")	Chi square

For percentages, use numerals before the % sign, as in 34%, but use the words percent or percentage when there is no number given, as in a large percentage.

When to Use Hyphens

Many statistics authors whose books are otherwise statistically sound do not use APA style. This makes their books poor choices for examples of correct formatting of statistical results and statistics in general when APA style is required. Even many of the statistics books written by psychologists do not conform completely to APA style.

It is quite common in statistics books and journals to see such terms as t-test, p-value (or P-value), z-score, and F-ratio used as nouns. The APA manual, however, informs us not to use a hyphen when these terms are used a nouns. Instead, you should write t test, p value, z score, and F ratio. When you use these terms as compound adjectives that precede the words they modify, you should use a hyphen, as in t-test results (APA, 2010, p. 100). However, when the terms follow the word they modify, you should not use a hyphen. To illustrate, you should write chi-square test of goodness of fit, but goodness-of-fit test.

Formatting Numbers

APA's general rule concerning numbers is to use numerals to express numbers 10 and above and words to express numbers below 10 (APA, 2010, p. 111). However, there are exceptions. Numerals should be used to express all numbers in the abstract of a paper or in a graphical display in the paper, and the numbers that precede a unit of measurement should be expressed in numerals, whether they are above or below 10. Numbers used to "represent statistical or mathematical functions, fractional or decimal quantities, percentages, ratios, and percentiles and quartiles" (APA, 2010, p. 111) should be expressed as numerals. Use numerals to express numbers that represent "time, dates, ages, scores and points on a scale, exact sums of money, and numbers as numerals" (APA, 2010, p. 112). Use words, however, to express numbers used as approximations of days, months, and years, as in about three years ago, but write 3 years of age.

Express numbers in words at the beginning of a sentence, or better yet, rewrite the sentence to avoid beginning with a number (APA, 2010, p. 112). Write common fractions such as one fifth and two-thirds majority in words (APA, 2010, p. 112). Use words for universally accepted usage such as the Seven Wonders of the Ancient World or the Twelve Apostles.

How Many Decimals to Report

The APA manual says that effective measures can generally be reported to two decimal places of accuracy. Statistics such as z, F, t, and χ^2 should always be formatted to two decimal places (APA, 2010, p. 114).

The former standard, and one still followed by many statistics authors, is to report probability values as p < .05 or p < .01, but the APA manual says now that you should report exact p values for both significant and nonsignificant results to two or three decimal places. This change is because modern statistical software makes it possible to determine precise probabilities. This new standard is stated in the APA manual (APA, 2010, p. 139). The < standard may still be needed in statistical tables, but in the text, the exact p value should be stated. Often, when the statistical software reports a very low probability, the significance level is shown as 0.000 or .000. Please note that this probability is not exactly zero, but is less than .001. In this case, the APA manual says to report p < .001 (APA, 2010, p. 139).

When numbers, such as correlation coefficients and p values, cannot exceed 1, APA says to omit the leading zero. When the number, such as a statistic, can exceed 1, you should include the leading zero. Thus you would write a z score of less than one as $z = 0.47$, but you would write $p = .037$.

What to Report

With a few exceptions, you should not include raw data in your paper, though you may want to make the raw data available via an online archive (APA, 2010, p. 32). Such data sharing is promoted by APA and other professional societies, and is a requirement for publication in certain journals. It is very instructive to study the sample papers in the APA manual to see how the statistical results should be formatted as well as the level of statistical detail that is generally used in research-based articles.

The APA manual instructs authors to include, as a minimum, the complete report of all hypothesis tests, estimates of appropriate effect sizes, and confidence intervals. It is not necessary to explain or interpret the effect-size estimates, as the APA manual tells us to assume our readers have a "professional knowledge of statistical methods" (APA, 2010, p. 33). It is sufficient to state the alpha level used (most commonly .05) once, and if all confidence intervals use the same confidence level, you can state that once as well.

Statistical results should include sample statistics such as the mean and standard deviation, and sample sizes. When you report the results of statistical tests, you should report the statistic, the degrees of freedom, the exact p value to two or three decimals, and an effect-size index. The APA manual also recommends that you report confidence intervals. The APA format for a confidence interval is XX% CI [LL, UL] where the XX is replaced by the confidence level, and the LL is replaced by the lower confidence limit and the UL is replaced by the upper confidence limit, as in 95% CI [28.47, 44.93].

Many statistics teachers require students to spell out the null and alternative hypotheses in both words and symbols and to specify whether the null hypothesis was rejected or not. These matters figure prominently in hypothesis tests, but APA style uses a shorthand way to state them. You should understand that when you state that a test of hypothesis is statistically significant, this is saying the same thing as to state that you have rejected the null hypothesis. This statement also implies that your results support the alternative or research hypothesis. However, in journals reporting research results, you will rarely see the hypotheses stated explicitly nor read that the researcher has rejected the null hypothesis. Instead, you will see an APA-style summary statement indicating that the test was significant or nonsignificant, followed by the p value and other information. This shorthand way of reporting statistical results is common in a number of fields, including most of the behavioral and social sciences, as well as business.

Examples of Statistical Results

The general rule of APA style is to report "sufficient information to allow the reader to fully understand the analyses conducted" (APA, 2010, p. 116) Statistical results should preferably be in the text, but depending on the magnitude of the data, possibly in an online data archive (APA, 2010, p. 116).

Below, I illustrate the correct way to report several common statistical tests by giving specific (and, I hope, interesting) examples. You can use these summary statements as a starting point for your own statements. Unless you have already taken statistics, you will not necessarily understand what all the symbols and statements mean, but this will serve as a general guideline for you, and you will understand the symbols and statements more if you have had stats or after you finish your statistics class. Your statistics instructors may ask you to included additional information, and you should obviously follow their instructions.

Reporting the Results of a *t* Test. The independent-samples *t* test is one of the most frequently used hypothesis tests. When you report the results of a *t* test, you should include the relevant sample statistics (in this case the means and standard deviations from which the value of t was calculated), the value of the test statistic, the degrees of freedom, the *p* value, an effect-size index (one of the most common ones is Cohen's *d*), and the relevant confidence interval. I found a data set online in which the midterm exam scores from two sections of the same introductory statistics course were displayed. The instructor taught the two sections by different means. One class was 100% online, and the other was taught by compressed video using interactive video conferencing. Here is how I would report the results of my independent-samples *t* test. Although it might be tempting to conclude that the online class performed better than the interactive video class, because the means are 81.70 and 77.89, respectively, we must do the hypothesis test before we can conclude anything. Because the variances are similar, I will use the *t* test that assumes equal variances in the population. Not all statisticians would agree with my choice here, and your instructor may prefer that you use the slightly more conservative test that does not assume equality of variance in the population. Regardless, here is how I would report that test:

An independent-samples t test assuming equality of variance showed that there was no significant difference between the midterm exam scores of the online class ($n = 46$, $M = 81.70$, $SD = 11.33$) and the interactive video class ($n = 35$, $M = 77.89$, $SD = 13.38$), $t(79) = 1.39$, $p = .17$, $d = 0.31$, 95% CI [−1.66, 9.28].

Study the example carefully and see that it provides the sample statistics and sample sizes, the value of the test statistic, the degrees of freedom, the *p* value, an effect-size index, and the confidence interval for the difference between the means. See that the confidence interval contains zero or no difference, which is another indication that the null hypothesis is not rejected. If the *p* value had been less than the predetermined alpha level (most commonly .05), the only difference in the statement would be that we would claim the means were significantly different.

Reporting the Results of an ANOVA. The analysis of variance (ANOVA) tests the differences among three or means. When you report the results of an ANOVA, you should give the sample sizes and summary statistics, the value of the *F* ratio, the degrees of freedom for the numerator and denominator terms, the *p* value, and an effect-size index. The most commonly reported effect-size index for the ANOVA is eta squared (or partial eta squared as illustrated above). Some statistical software calculates eta squared for you, but many programs do not. If you need to calculate it, it is simply the treatment sum of squares divided by the total sum of squares. The effect-size index in this case gives us a percentage of the total variation in the dependent variable that can be explained by knowledge of the independent variable. If there is a significant main effect, you should interpret it, and often it is helpful to do post hoc comparisons to determine which means differ significantly from others. If you have a higher order ANOVA and there are significant interactions of two or more independent variables, you should examine and interpret these before examining main effects, and before doing any post hoc comparisons, which may be inappropriate if the interaction plots a "disordinal" set of lines (lines that cross each other). Although it is not customary to display graphs of mean plots and interactions in published articles, they may be quite helpful in student papers for clarity.

As an example of analysis of variance, the following data set came from one of my business statistics books. Each of fifteen identical cars is randomly assigned to one of three groups (see Table 2). Each car is then driven the same distance and the same speed on a machine called a dynamometer that simulates the driving environment and records the exact gasoline mileage. Each group of vehicles uses a different brand of gasoline, and the following highway mileages are recorded:

Table 2. Gasoline mileage for three brands of fuel

Brand A	Brand B	Brand C
34.0	35.3	33.3
35.0	36.5	34.0
34.3	36.4	34.7
35.5	37.0	33.0
35.8	37.6	34.9

The significant one-way ANOVA followed by a Tukey HSD (honestly significant difference) test would be reported in a fashion similar to this:

A one-way analysis of variance demonstrated a significant difference among the highway gasoline mileage means of brands A (M = 34.92, SD = 0.77), B (M = 36.56, SD = 0.85), and C (M = 33.98, SD = 0.70), $F(2, 12)$ = 12.74, p = .001, η^2 = .68. Post hoc comparisons using the Tukey HSD criterion indicated that Brand A produced significantly lower gasoline mileage than Brand B, p = .02, 95% CI [0.26, 3.02]. Brands A and B did not differ significantly, p = .206, 95% CI [–2.32, 0.44]. Brand C also produced lower gasoline mileage than Brand B, p = .001, 95% CI [–3.96, –1.20].

The F tests in ANOVA are technically two-tailed even though you place all of the alpha level in the right tail of the F distribution, and are reporting a one-tailed p value. The reason for this is the statistical and mathematical relationship between the theoretical t distribution and the F distribution. The F distribution with two groups is the equivalent of the square of the t distribution (Rosnow, Rosenthal, & Rubin, 2000), and the p value for the F ratio in an ANOVA with two groups will be exactly the same as the p value for a two-tailed t test for the same two groups. Remember that the F ratio is based on squared deviations, and both positive and negative differences between means will produce positive squared deviations and thus increase the value of F.

Reporting the Results of a Chi-Square Test. Chi-square tests compare observed and expected frequencies in two or more categories under some specific null hypothesis. There are two kinds of chi-square tests, one of which is the goodness of fit test, and the other of which is the test of independence. For goodness of fit tests, we are working with one sample, and with independence tests, we are working with two categorical variables.

When reporting chi-square tests, you must give both the sample size and the degrees of freedom, because the degrees of freedom are based on the number of categories, not the sample size. You should report the value of chi-square, the p value, and an effect-size index. For chi-square tests of independence, the most commonly reported effect-size index is Cramér's V or the phi coefficient for tests from a two-way 2 × 2 contingency table, which will produce a test with one degree of freedom. Most statistical software will calculate and report the effect-size index if you ask for it. The chi-square test is often called Pearson's Chi-Square because it is a result of the work of statistician Karl Pearson. Technically, APA style would literally tell us to use chi square as a noun and reserve chi-square for a compound adjective, but most statisticians use chi-square as both a noun and an adjective, and I typically do that as well, for consistency. According to the APA rules, you would write chi square distribution, chi-square test of goodness of fit, and chi-square goodness-of-fit test.

An interesting application of the chi-square goodness-of-fit test involves the distribution of numbers. Although one might think intuitively that the numbers 1–9 occur with equal frequencies, this is often not true. A physicist named Benford discovered that the leading digits of many kinds of data sets are not uniformly distributed, but distributed in the following fashion (Table 3):

Table 3. Benford's Distribution

Leading Digit	Percentage
1	30.1%
2	17.6%
3	12.5%
4	9.7%
5	7.9%
6	6.7%
7	5.8%
8	5.1%
9	4.6%

Researchers have found that financial and accounting data in particular are well described by Benford's law, and this observation has allowed auditors to detect fraud because fraudulent numbers are unlikely to follow Benford's law. Consider the following hypothetical data (based on Durtsci, Hillison, & Pacini, 2004). An auditor obtained a sample of 288 checks written by an insurance refund account officer. Here is the distribution of the leading digits of the checks. The expected frequencies are derived simply by multiplying the total number of checks by the proportions shown in the Benford distribution (Table 4).

Table 4. Hypothetical fraudulent check data

Leading Digit	Actual	Expected
1	132	86.7
2	50	50.7
3	32	36.0
4	20	27.9
5	19	22.8
6	11	19.3
7	10	16.7
8	9	14.7
9	5	13.2

The chi-square test was significant, indicating that fraud was likely. Here is how you might report a chi-square goodness-of-fit test.

A chi-square test of goodness of fit revealed that the actual first digits of the checks were significantly different from the expected distribution under Benford's law, $\chi^2(8, N = 288) = 40.55, p < .001$.

Further investigation by the auditor led to the conclusion that the refund officer had established bogus shell companies in her own name and was writing large checks to these companies. An unexpectedly large number of these checks were in amounts just over $1,000. Approximately $80,000 had been diverted to the shell companies before the fraud was detected (Durtsci, Hillison, & Pacini, 2004, p. 31).

For a chi-square test of independence, the only addition to the above information would be an effect-size index.

Reporting the Results of Correlation and Regression. In correlational analyses, we determine the strength and direction of the linear relationship between two continuous variables. In regression analysis, we determine the coefficients of the regression equation and test them for significance. These are widely used techniques in a variety of research projects and applied situations such as human resource selection, forecasting, econometrics, and educational research.

As with other statistics, you should report correlation coefficients to two decimal places of accuracy. When reporting regression coefficients, you should also report those to two decimal places. The p value for the correlation coefficient and the regression coefficients should be reported to two or three decimals as appropriate. These same rules apply for multiple regression. For correlation, the square of the correlation coefficient (known as the coefficient of determination) is a widely-accepted effect-size index, and represents the percentage of variation shared by the dependent variable and the independent variable(s).

Remember that correlation coefficients cannot exceed 1, so the leading zero should not be reported, but regression coefficients can exceed 1, so when these are reported, the leading zero should be included when their values are less than 1. Correlational analyses often are reported in tables, and in such cases, the use of the $p <$ style may be helpful. The APA manual gives the following example of a correlation matrix for two different samples (see Table 5, adapted from APA, 2010, p. 136):

Table 5. Correlation matrix for two samples (adapted from APA, 2010)

Measure	1	2	3	4	M	SD
BSS	—	.54*	.29*	−.23*	1.31	4.32
BDI	.54*	—	.34*	−.14*	8.33	7.76
SAFE	.19*	.30*	—	−.07	47.18	13.24
MEIM	−.09	−.11	−.05	—	47.19	6.26
M	1.50	9.13	39.07	37.78		
SD	3.84	7.25	13.17	7.29		

*$p <$ .01.

Examine the correct format for a table in APA style. In the text, we would report p values to two or three decimal places (APA, 2010, p. 139) but we might revert to the $p <$ style if the use of exact probabilities would make it difficult to comprehend the table. If you are reporting the correlation matrix for a single sample, note that the values above the diagonal will be the same as those below the diagonal because of the symmetry of the correlation matrix, and many authors use the lower part of the matrix to report sample sizes (or degrees of freedom) or exact p values.

When you report correlation results in your text, the format is similar to that for other statistics. For example, in a recent study of student and faculty members' attitudes toward plagiarism and other forms of cheating (Pace, 2012), I noted that respondents who thought students plagiarize because they are lazy also believed that students thought they would get away with their cheating, $r = .42, p = .001$. The slope of the regression line was significant, $b = 0.37, F(1,54) = 11.71, p = .001$, 95% CI [0.15, 0.59].

Looking Ahead

In Chapter 7, we step away from APA style and Word to discuss some of the common writing errors students (and faculty members) make, and you will learn how to correct or avoid these mistakes in your own writing. I also show you how to adjust Word's Review options to make them more helpful.

Chapter 7—Writing Errors to Avoid

In this chapter, we digress momentarily from Word and APA style to talk about some of the most common writing errors I see in student papers. We have already addressed formatting issues, including page headers, spacing, references, and in-text citations. But we will now look more deeply at a few sticky issues that cause students to lose points on their papers. We have addressed some of these errors previously, but important lessons bear repeating. At the end of the chapter, you will learn how to modify Word's settings to give you more and better feedback about your writing and its readability.

What is Good Writing?

The reason English is a required subject both for native speakers and for those for whom it is a second language is that "nothing in your education is more important than learning how to express yourself well" (Warriner, 1988, p. ix). English is a difficult language to master and has more rules and exceptions than many other languages. Before addressing writing errors, let us discuss what good writing involves with regard to research papers.

Writing a research paper is different from other kinds of writing. When I was in high school and college many years ago, the use of index cards and notes was a good way to manage sources and plan a document. I took typing in high school, working on a manual typewriter. Now, you can use your computer for these purposes. Some things, however, have changed very little over the years. Though it is easier than ever to use technology to produce documents, good writing still requires work, revision, careful editing, and close proofreading. Although there are many talented writers, anyone can become a better writer by following some very simple guidelines. In a planning and writing a research paper, you need to master the following twelve steps (adapted from Warriner, 1988, p. xviii):

1. Selecting a suitable subject. In many courses, you have the flexibility to choose your topic, while in many others, the topic will be assigned to you.
2. Developing a purpose statement.
3. Developing a preliminary outline. Word can help here, too, though we will not discuss it much further in this text. Remember one of the views you can use in Word is the Outline view (See Figure 50 for the Outline view of this page).
4. Locating suitable sources and gathering information. Remember the gold standard for academic research papers is peer-reviewed articles in scholarly journals.
5. Compiling a working reference list.
6. Preparing the final outline.
7. Writing a first draft.
8. Documenting sources with in-text citations and a reference list.
9. Incorporating quotations (be very judicious here).
10. Revising the draft.
11. Preparing the final copy.
12. Preparing the final reference list.

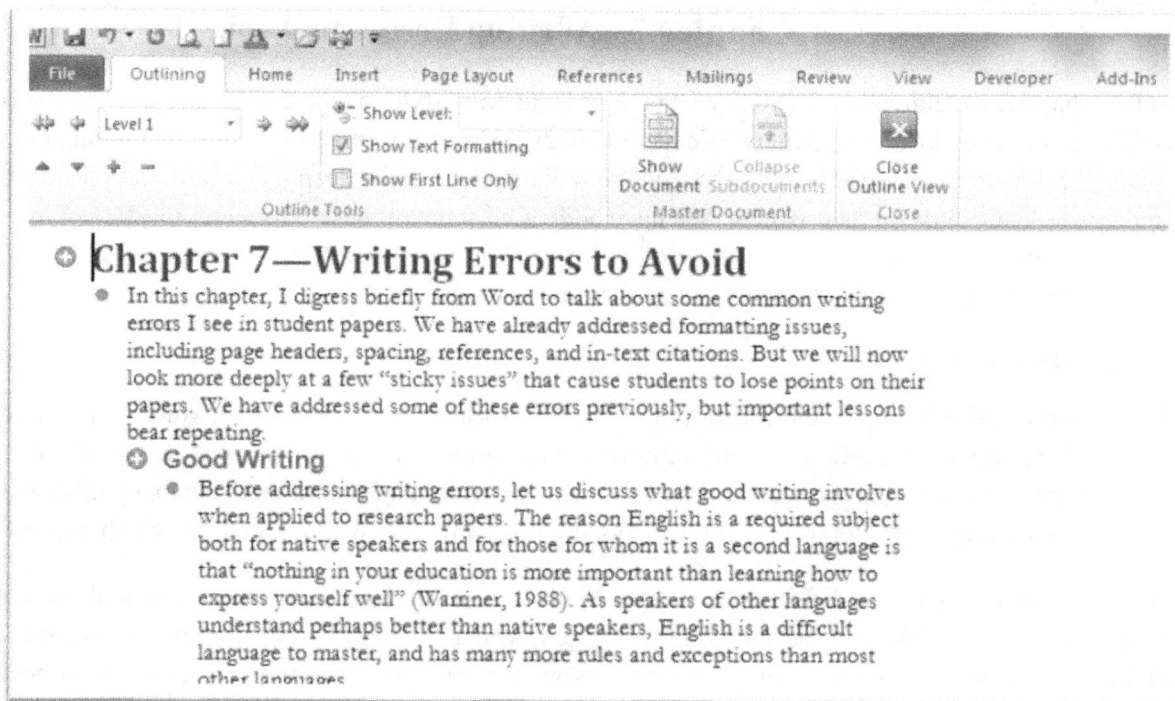

Figure 50. Outline view in Word 2010

You may be thinking, "But my paper needs to be only five pages long! Why would I want to do all those 12 things for a five-page paper?" In my experience, many students instead simply start writing and quit when they reach the minimum page limit, use Google and Wikipedia as their primary "research" tools, quote excessively, often plagiarize, tack on the minimum number of required references, and never revise their papers. The result is unsurprisingly often something unimaginative, uninformative, and even unintelligible.

Here is an actual quote from a graduate student's paper. I can bet the student either never learned the steps above, or if he did, did not follow them in writing this paper. This is not the worst example I have seen, but it is clearly not good writing.

> "The three examples that I would like to use of knowledge management is as follows; identifies, creativity and distribution of products and plans, that will continue the growth and success in the organization."

Good writing may appear effortless, but it is usually the result of a great deal of hard work, revision, and skill. Being a talented writer is a wonderful thing for those lucky enough to be so gifted, but being a good writer is within the reach of anyone willing to work, accept criticism, and learn from his or her mistakes.

Scientific Writing Versus Creative Writing

Like many composition texts, the APA manual reminds us scientific writing is different from creative writing. Creative writing often involves devices such as the use of ambiguity, omission of the expected and insertion of the unexpected, and sudden shifts in topic, tense, or person (APA, 2010, p. 65). In scientific writing, however, you should avoid these devices. The aim is "clear and logical communication" (APA, 2010, p. 65). According to the *Little, Brown Compact Handbook* (Aaron, 2011), academic writing should be authoritative and its tone should be neutral.

Use the past tense or the past perfect tense (research showed or research has shown) for the literature review and the description of the procedure and results. On the other hand, use the present tense to discuss the implications of the results and your conclusions (APA, 2010, p. 66).

Avoid wordiness and practice economy of expression (APA, 2010, p. 67). Many writers use redundancy in an effort to be emphatic. APA says you should use no more words than are necessary (APA, 2010, p. 67). For example, change a combined total of 68 participants to 68 participants.

When you proofread your paper before submitting it, ask yourself if there are any words that add no value. Many words and phrases are fillers adding no value to the paper, and taking unnecessary space. For example, each and every can be replaced by writing either each or every, but both together are redundant.

Raimes (2004, pp. 590-621) offers writing advice in the form of Five Cs:

The first C is *Cut*. Cut wordiness and repetition, as discussed above. Cut formulaic phrases. For example, many writers rely on stock phrases to get their writing going or to keep it flowing. Some common phrases are at the present time (try now), are of the opinion (try believe), last but not least (try finally), and concerning the matter of (use about). According to Aaron (2011), you should cut out "empty words" that add no value to your paper. Examples include such formulaic phrases as "all things considered, as far as I am concerned, for all intents and purposes, last but not least, and more or less." You can also substitute a single word for many stock phrases, such as "at all times" (try always), and "due to the fact that" (try because). When you are rewriting, eliminate the formulaic phrases. For example, while I am drafting text, I often write, "please note" or "note that" as devices to keep my train of thought going. But when I revise, I use the find and replace features of Word to eliminate most of those, as they typically add little or no value. It is rarely if ever necessary to say "the fact that." Just cut it out. When you edit your final draft, remove every unnecessary word and phrase.

You should also cut references to your intentions. Rather than saying "This paper describes three approaches to classifying research," or "In this paper, I will describe three approaches to classifying research," you can just say, "Three approaches to classifying research are…" Cut redundant words and phrases such as advance planning, refer back, free gift, and cooperate together (Raimes, 2004, p. 594). Finally, cut material quoted unnecessarily (Raimes, 2004, p. 595). We will discuss this in more detail at the end of this chapter.

The second C is *Check for Action*. It is much stronger to use active voice than passive voice. We discuss the use of active voice more extensively below.

The third C is *Connect*. Connect your ideas by consistent subjects and topic chains (Raimes, 2004, p. 602). Use transition to make your writing flow. Place important information near the end of a paragraph for emphasis.

The fourth C is *Commit*. Your papers should reflect your commitment to an informed and interesting point of view—and not necessarily the dominant one (Raimes, 2004, p. 612).

The fifth C is *Choose Your Words*. Even in the modern era of technology, dictionaries and thesauruses are useful tools. There are review tools built into Word that allow you to find online dictionaries and thesauruses as well. Find these tools by clicking on **Review** > **Proofing** (Figure 51).

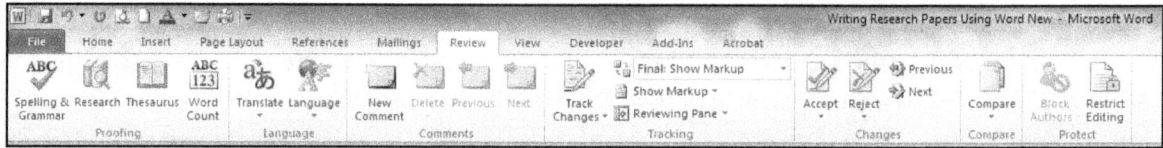

Figure 51.Accessing the Proofing Group on the Review tab

Using Incorrect Labels, Abbreviations, and Symbols

Many students label the running head incorrectly, as we discussed earlier. The most unusual one I have seen recently was "Running Headline." That is creative, but incorrect. Students also format their titles incorrectly, sometimes putting them in boldface, and sometimes using underlining or italics or quotation marks. As we discussed, students also have a variety of creative but incorrect ways of labeling their reference list ranging from putting References: with a colon at the left margin or centered, to using labels such as Resources, Works Cited, Sources, or Bibliography.

Students often use pg. to abbreviate page. The APA abbreviation for page is p. (with the period). The APA abbreviation for pages is pp. (with the period). In the previous version of the APA manual (APA, 2001), authors were instructed to use either the abbreviation para. (with the period) or the actual paragraph symbol (¶), but with the new version of the manual, we are told to use only the abbreviation para. (APA, 2010).

Remember the APA abbreviation for edition is ed. The abbreviation for editor is Ed. When you provide the edition number, the parenthetical information should not be in italics, even though the book title should be. If you use the bibliographic tools as we discussed in Chapter 5, you will find that you can get this right every time when you use the tool properly.

Problems with Italics, Bolding, Quotation Marks, and Punctuation

Many students use punctuation incorrectly. Some students use boldface and italics for mere emphasis, but the APA manual says not to do that. I have even had students who typed their entire papers in italics because they liked the way it looked.

Commas and periods usually go inside quotation marks rather than after them, but many students put them after the quotation marks. Most other forms of punctuation come after the quotation marks unless they are part of the quoted material. Commas and periods are used to separate parts of references and citations, but when two or more references are cited in the text in the same set of parentheses, semicolons should separate these citations. Punctuation problems are often combined with other problems, so I will discuss several common problems and show the correct way to format your papers to avoid them.

Many writers like to omit a comma before the word and in a list or series. Although that is commonly accepted practice and a matter of personal preference, the APA manual says that you should put a comma before the last element. "Use a comma between elements (include before and and or) in a series of three or more items" (APA, 2010, p. 88).

Examine the sentence immediately preceding this one. See that when an in-text citation occurs at the end of a sentence, the period should come after the citation, not before it, and there should be no punctuation of any kind before the closing quotation mark. See the follow examples.

Example 1: This is incorrect:

The APA manual says, "Use a comma between elements (include before and and or) in a series of three or more items." (APA, 2010, p. 88).

Example 2: This is also incorrect:

The APA manual says, "Use a comma between elements (include before and and or) in a series of three or more items." (APA, 2010, p. 88)

Example 3: This is also incorrect:

The APA manual says, "Use a comma between elements (include before and and or) in a series of three or more items," (APA, 2010, p. 88).

This rule is true whether or not the sentence ends with quoted material. There should be no additional punctuation inside the quotation marks in this particular case. If the sentence ends with a citation but not with a quote, the period should come after the parentheses, and not before them. After problems with the running head, this is the second most common mistakes in student papers. Many students put the period at the end of the sentence as shown in Example 2 above, but this leaves the erroneous impression that the citation goes with the next sentence, not the previous one.

A related problem is knowing when and how to use quotation marks. As I mentioned earlier, any quote of fewer than 40 words should be included in your narrative. When you quote directly in your text, you must enclose the words of others in quotation marks. You must include an in-text citation showing the author and date along with the page number from which you took this material. You must also include a reference list entry showing how your reader can obtain the same source. When the document (such as a web page) does not have page numbers, you should cite the paragraph number if that is available, and if not, you should cite the section title and the paragraph number. The APA manual contains specific instructions for dealing with quoted material when the page numbers are not available.

As we also discussed earlier, if the quoted material is 40 or more words in length, it should be set off as a block quote. For block quotes, you should not use quotation marks, and you should close the last sentence with a period before citing the source at the end.

Common Sticking Points

Here are some of the things many students find difficult to master.

Using & and "And" Incorrectly. A curious aspect of APA style is that when you are typing in the body of your document, you should spell out the word *and*. This includes in-text citations such as Rosnow and Rosnow (1986). But when you are using parentheses, you should use the ampersand symbol (&) instead of writing out *and*, as in (Rosnow & Rosnow, 1986). In the reference list, you separate multiple authors' names by commas, even when there are only two authors, and you precede the second or last author's name by & instead of the word *and*. I have shown this format throughout this document, but it is something many students get wrong. As with many of the APA rules, this is something you simply have to memorize and follow.

Spacing Problems. Remember the following rules. Use one space between p. and the page number, as in p. 32. Use one space after a colon, comma, or semicolon. Put one space between an author's initials in the text and in the reference list. In the body of your text, use two spaces after a sentence. Sentences can be terminated by a period, a question mark, or an exclamation point. Do not put two spaces after a period used to separate parts of a reference entry. Do not put extra spacing in internal abbreviations like n.d. or U.S.

Use of Contractions. Many students use contractions in their papers. Although this is not addressed in the APA manual, academic writing guides instruct you to avoid contractions in formal writing.

A related problem is that many students confuse its and it's. Note that its is possessive and does not need an apostrophe. On the other hand, it's is the contraction for it is. If you have trouble knowing the difference, just read the sentence aloud and change its or it's to it is and see if it fits. If it does, you should be using it's. If it does not, then you should probably use its. For example, I often have lunch at a local restaurant with a menu proudly proclaiming they serve *"Good Food at It's Finest."* If you change this to "Good Food at It Is Finest," that make no sense. Remember to avoid the use of contractions in your formal writing unless they are part of quoted material. I am happy to report that the restaurant just changed its (not it's) signage and menu to its, not it's!

Since and Because. Many writers and speakers use the word *since* to mean because, perhaps saying (or writing) something like, "Since he is stubborn, he refuses to listen to me." The APA manual recommends that the word since be used only in reference to time, as in "It has been three days since I last saw you." The fifth edition of the APA manual (2001) was more instructive than the sixth edition (2010) in many matters concerning writing style. According to the fifth edition, "Some style authorities accept the use of *while* and *since* when they do not refer strictly to time; however, words like these, with more than one meaning, can cause confusion" (APA, 2001, p. 56), and *"Since* is more precise when it is used to refer only to time (to mean 'after that'); otherwise replace it with *because"* (APA, 2001, p. 57). The newer APA manual gives us the same instruction (APA, 2010, p. 84).

Hopefully. Hopefully means "in a hopeful manner" or "full of hope" (APA, 2001, p. 54). It is incorrect to write, "Hopefully, I will see you soon." Instead, you should write, "I hope to see you soon." You can say, "I am waiting hopefully," but hopefully should not be used to mean "I hope" or "it is hoped" (APA, 2001, p. 54).

Allot of Everyday Problems. When something happens every day, you should write *every* and *day* as separate words. You would say that the alarm clock goes off every day, rather than everyday. Many students write *alot*, rather than a lot. Remember that *allot* means to allocate, that a *lot* is, well, a lot (as in a parking lot or a large quantity), and that alot is not a word. It is also imprecise to use a lot to refer to quantity, and in scientific writing, you should generally avoid the term.

That and Which. It is common in written and spoken English to use *that* and *which* interchangeably, but the APA manual says to use *that* with restrictive clauses and *which* with nonrestrictive clauses. A restrictive clause is necessary to the meaning of the sentence, while a nonrestrictive one is not essential, and may simply add additional information. You should set off nonrestrictive clauses with commas (APA, 2010, p. 83), but you should not use a comma before a restrictive clause.

Many speakers and writers refer to people as *that*, but APA instructs writers to use *who* for human beings and that or which for nonhuman animals and things (APA, 2010, p. 79).

Use of Third Person. Although many writing instructors and professors tell you to refer to yourself in the third person in your formal writing, the APA manual instructs you to refer to yourself as I or me when self-reference is necessary (APA 2010, p. 69). Good writers know that excessive self-reference is distracting, and they generally avoid it. I am breaking my own rule here because I am intentionally writing this book in a conversational tone, but I would not write this way in a research paper, a report, or a more academic book.

This subject was addressed more thoroughly in the fifth edition of the APA manual (APA, 2001) than it is in the new sixth edition (APA, 2010), but both are clear that when you refer to yourself as the author, the writer, or the researcher, this makes your writing unclear. Simply refer to yourself in the first person when necessary, and avoid self-reference as much as possible.

Getting the Number Wrong. It is quite common in currently spoken and written English to refer to a person as *they* or *their*. For example, someone might write, "A student should explore *their* options carefully." This is technically incorrect because a *student* is singular and they and *their* is plural. You can fix this in a couple of different ways. Although it is awkward, you could say correctly, "A student should explore *his or her* options carefully." To say, "A student should explore *his* options carefully" implies that students are all males, which is not true. Another and better way to fix this problem is to say *"Students* should examine *their* options carefully." This avoids the awkward "his or her" construction, and is also grammatically correct.

Regarding "Regards." This is a pet peeve with me. I hear educated people say *"in regards to this or that."* But *regards* are friendly greetings showing respect and affection. In both spoken and written English, many speakers and writers use, *"In regards to,"* when referring to something. This is considered substandard English (Wilson, 1993), and you should not use "in regards to" or "with regards to" in your speech or your writing, unless you are wishing someone well, as in "with warm regards to you and your family."

When referring to something, *to regard* means our *attention* or *consideration*. Instead of saying "in regards to," you could say "as regards," "in regard to," or "regarding," or you can use other words such as "concerning" or "with reference to."

Using Fancy or Foreign Words When Plain Words Work Better. *"If desired behaviors are linked to reinforcing stimuli, the probability that the desired behavior will be repeated naturally in the future skyrockets."*

This was written by a student in a master's level course. Although the sentence is grammatically correct, it is confusing and has an interesting alternative interpretation. I was surprised to contemplate that desired behavior will occur naturally in the skyrockets of the future. I can hardly wait! I suggested the student just say, "Behaviors that are reinforced are likely to be repeated," which is what I think she really meant to say. Remember good writing is intended to express, and not to impress.

You can ask Word to give you the reading index of your document, and I recommend you do that. Use the simplest words needed to make your points. It does not make your paper better to use fancy or foreign words, especially if you are not sure you understand them or know how to spell them. I have students write *viola* instead of *voilà*, *chow* instead of *ciao*, and *foh pah* instead of *faux pas*. One student wrote me to explain she had committed a *"foh pah,"* and indeed she had. Using such words incorrectly does leave an impression on your readers, but not the one you intended.

Many simple words are underused, and other words that mean the same thing are overused or unnecessary when a simpler word is available. For example, the word *utilize* means the same thing as *use*. *Legitimatize* or *legitimize* both mean the same thing as the verb to *legitimate*. Although many students like to write *"amongst,"* *among* works just as well, and sounds less pretentious.

In a similar vein, writers should avoid stuffiness. Formal does not mean "stuffy and pretentious" (Raimes, 2004, p. 631). For example instead of writing ascertain, just write find out. Instead of optimal, write best. Use carry out instead of implement, and begin instead of commence.

Excessive Reliance on Passive Voice. You should develop a habit of writing in the forcible active voice. This is as true for scientific writing as for any other kind (Strunk, 1918). Students often write sentences such as the following: "The reason that he left college was that his health became impaired" (Strunk, 1918, para. 11). But note how much stronger it is to say, "Failing health compelled him to leave college" (Strunk, 1918, para.11).

Passive voice is sometimes useful because we want to be tactful or precise, but generally, passive voice is far weaker than active voice. You can ask Word to check for the use of passive voice when you review your document, and I recommend you do. When you write in passive voice, your writing is less effective than when you write in active voice. It is also very often unclear who the actor is when you use passive voice. Instead of saying, "My first trip to England will always be remembered," try "I will always remember my first trip to England." In the first sentence, it is not clear who will do the remembering. Will it be I, my family, or the startled English citizens who heard my Southern U.S. drawl? Instead of saying, "It was decided that leaders would receive training," you can say more directly, "The executives decided that leaders would receive training." It is even worse to say, "It was decided by the executives that training would be received by the leaders."

Excessive Use of Quotation. This is another pet peeve. According to many of my students, instructors often encourage students to quote extensively from their sources, presumably to show that the student actually read the source. Excessive quotation, however, is a very weak form of writing, and has been called "*lazy writing*" (Rosnow & Rosnow, 1986, p. 28).

Even when you cite the source of the quoted material, the excessive use of quoted material is only one step above outright plagiarism, because you are letting the words of others fill your paper. Excessive quotations are distracting. You do not display any creativity or critical thinking when you use excessive quotation, and your own voice is lost in the process. It is far more effective to summarize and paraphrase your sources, while still citing them to give others credit for their ideas.

Changing Word's Review Settings

Here is how to set the Review options in Word to include self-reference and passive voice, and to give you the reading index for your document. Click on **File** > **Options** > **Proofing**. Find the section labeled When correcting spelling and grammar in Word (see Figure 52)

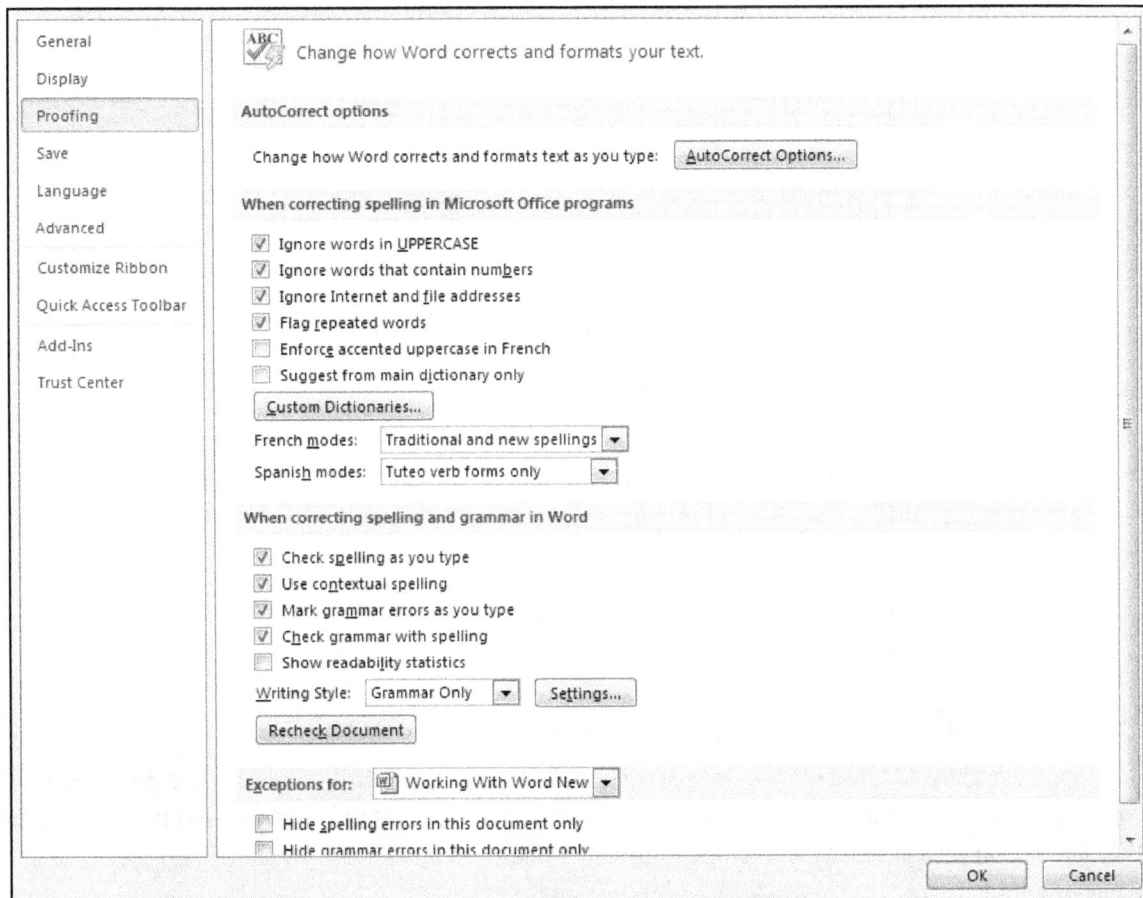

Figure 52. Changing Word's Review settings

Click on Settings. Here is the dialog (Figure 53). Scroll down to Style. I recommend you check the boxes in front of Clichés, Colloquialisms, and Jargon; Contractions; Passive sentences; and Use of first person (you will have to scroll farther down to see that option). I also recommend you check the box in front of Show readability statistics.

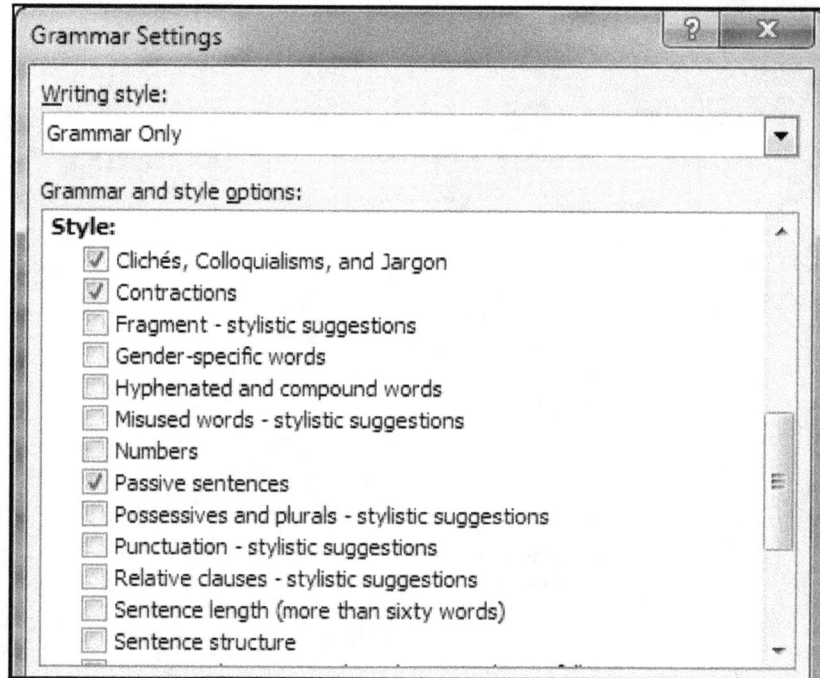

Figure 53. Changing Word's grammar settings

Here is the Spelling & Grammar review of this book in an earlier draft stage (Figure 54). I learned by examining it that I needed to cut down on the number of words per sentence, but I was pleased the reading level was grade 10.1. I was also pleased that the average number of characters per word was only 4.6, because I want the book to be easy to read.

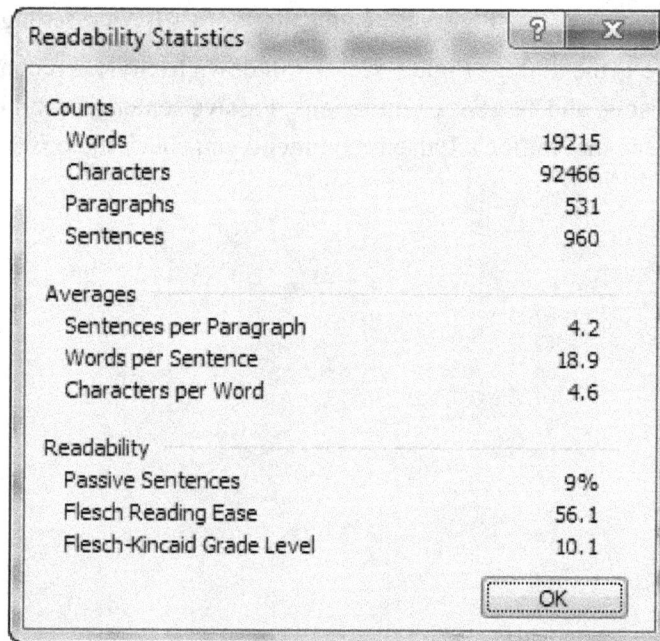

Figure 54. Readability analysis of a draft of this book

Below is the readability analysis of the final copy of the book. See that I managed to reduce the occurrence of passive voice, the number of sentences per paragraph, and the number of words per sentence. I was also able to reduce the difficulty level of the text, writing at a level that makes the book accessible to virtually all readers with a high school education (Figure 55).

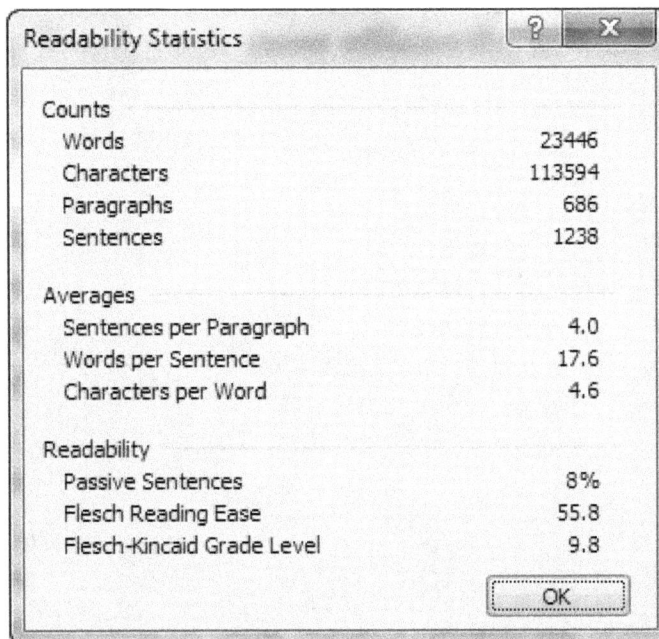

Figure 55. The readability analysis of the final copy of this text

Looking Ahead

The final chapter of this book covers the creation of the long-awaited APA style template. By following the instructions in Chapter 8, you will be able to create and save your own APA template, which will automate everything but the actual content of your papers.

Chapter 8—Creating a Document Template

Now that we have covered formatting and writing your paper, let us turn our attention to building an APA style document template you can use for all your papers. We will use the example paper from Chapter 3 as our guide. If you try unsuccessfully to create the APA style document template, you can e-mail me at larry@twopaces.com, and I will e-mail you a copy of my personal APA style template that will work in any version of Word from 2003 to the present.

Creating a Template

To create a new template, simply launch Word to open a new blank document. We will modify the styles and add one style. We will set the default text to Times New Roman 12-point font, and the default line spacing to double spacing. When the template is finished, we will save it as a Word template. After that, you will be able to access the template whenever you need to write a new paper, and you will not have to do anything other than make a few changes such as editing the title and the page headers before you begin typing away. Our template will include styles for two levels of headings, titles, the normal text (the body of the document), and the reference list. These will have the correct margins preset.

As discussed above, your college or university probably has additional requirements for the cover page, so you should follow the guidance provided to you for those requirements. If your instructor does not require an abstract, you can simply delete page 2, and the template will fix your page numbers automatically. When you add new pages, they will be formatted and numbered correctly.

First, save the document as a template file. To do that, select **File** > **Save As** and give your template a descriptive name. I chose "APA Style Template" as the name of my file (without the quotes, obviously). Under Save as type, select Word Template from the dropdown list (see Figure 56).

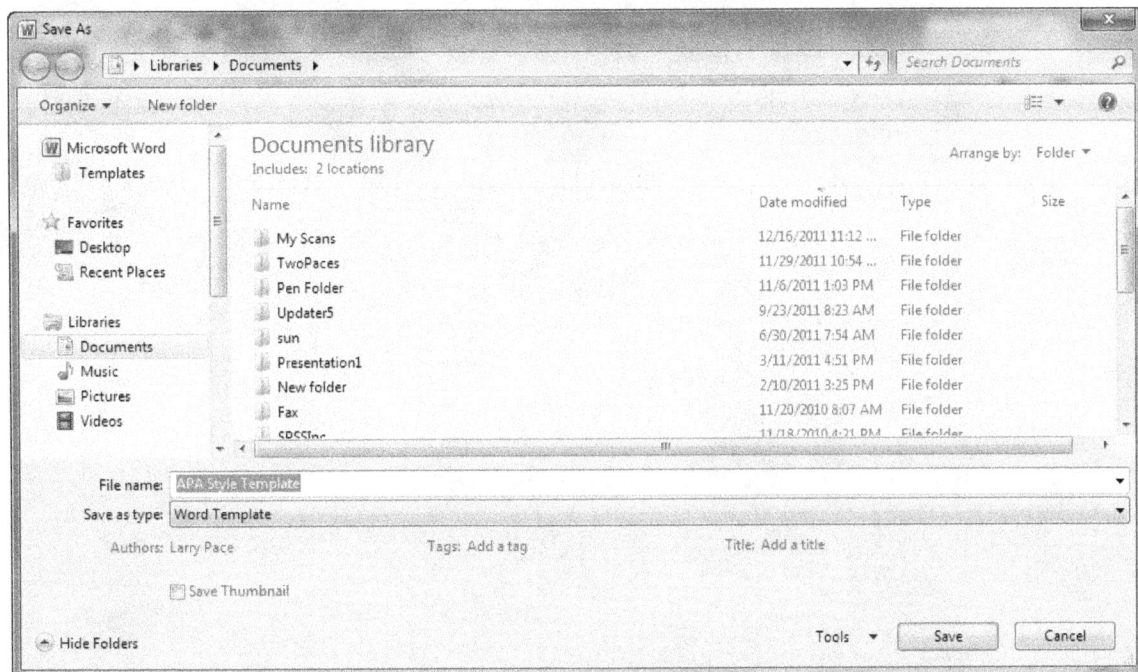

Figure 56. Saving a file as a template

Next, let us set the default text (Normal style) to Times New Roman 12-point font with double spacing. Find **Home** > **Styles** > **Normal**. Right click and select Modify. You can change the font, the spacing, and other features directly from the next dialog box, or you can click on the Format button at the bottom to access individual features, if you prefer. You should not use full justification for your papers. Instead, leave the right margin "ragged."

Select New documents based on this template. Now, any document you create when you use this template will have the correct style for the normal text, including the page headers and numbers.

Now, let us modify Heading 1 and Heading 2 to match APA style. Because the default headings have unusual formatting, the easiest way to do this is to format some text in the style you desire and then update the style you want to use that formatting. As we have discussed and illustrated that previously, I will not show all the screen captures. Remember Level 1 headings should be in Times New Roman 12-point font, bolded, and centered. Level 2 headings should be in Times New Roman 12-point font, bolded, and at the left margin.

Change the Title style to Times New Roman 12-point regular font. Remember the titles on the cover page and the top of page 3 (or page 2 if you are not using an abstract), the word Abstract, and the word References should not be in boldface. These titles should be centered. The default title style will have some additional spacing and use expanded font, to it really better to create the correct format in your document and then modify the style as we discussed earlier.

We can now add a style for the References. To create a new style, find the little launch dialog icon at the bottom right of the Styles group. Click there and note the button to create a new style at the bottom (Figure 57).

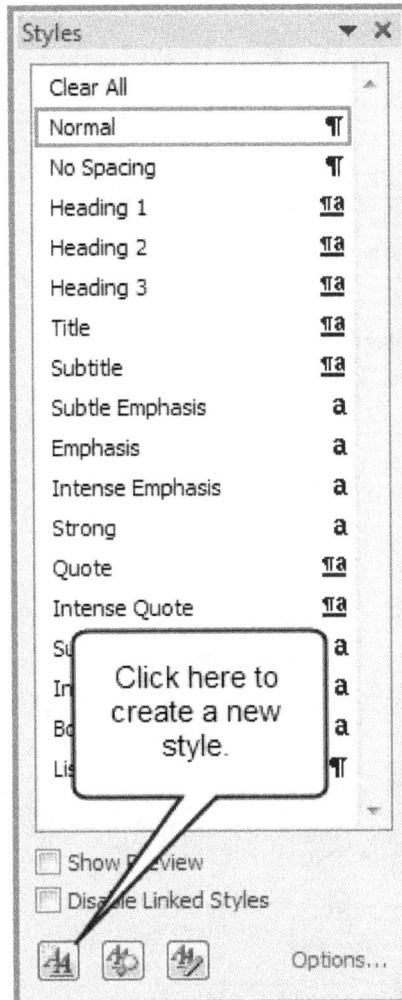

Figure 57. Creating a new style

Specify the new style with the word References and select "based on Normal." Click on the Format button and access the paragraph dialog. Change the indentation to a .5 inch hanging indent (see Figure 58).

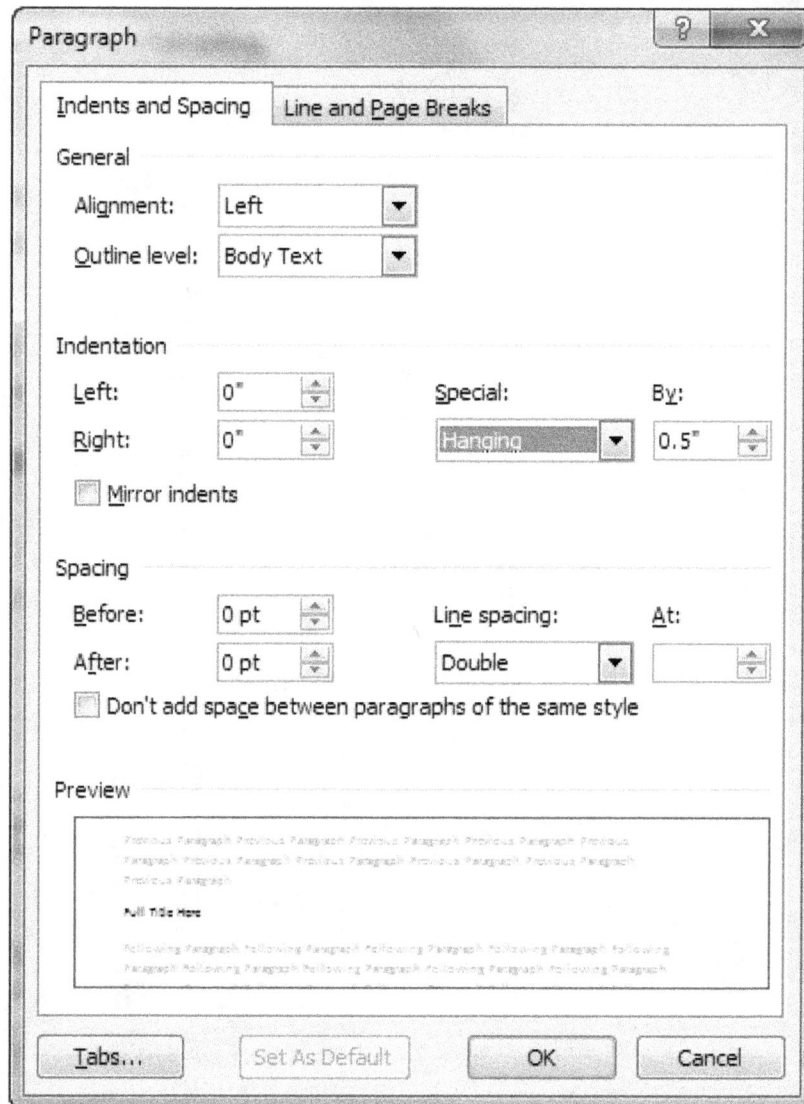

Figure 58. Specifying spacing and indentation options for the new style

All our modified styles will now apply to new documents based on this template. To make it easier to use, go ahead and add the page headers and numbers, a page for the abstract, a page for the body text, and a page for the reference list. As a placeholder, I will insert the reference to the APA manual there. Here is page 1 (the cover page) of our completed template (Figure 59):

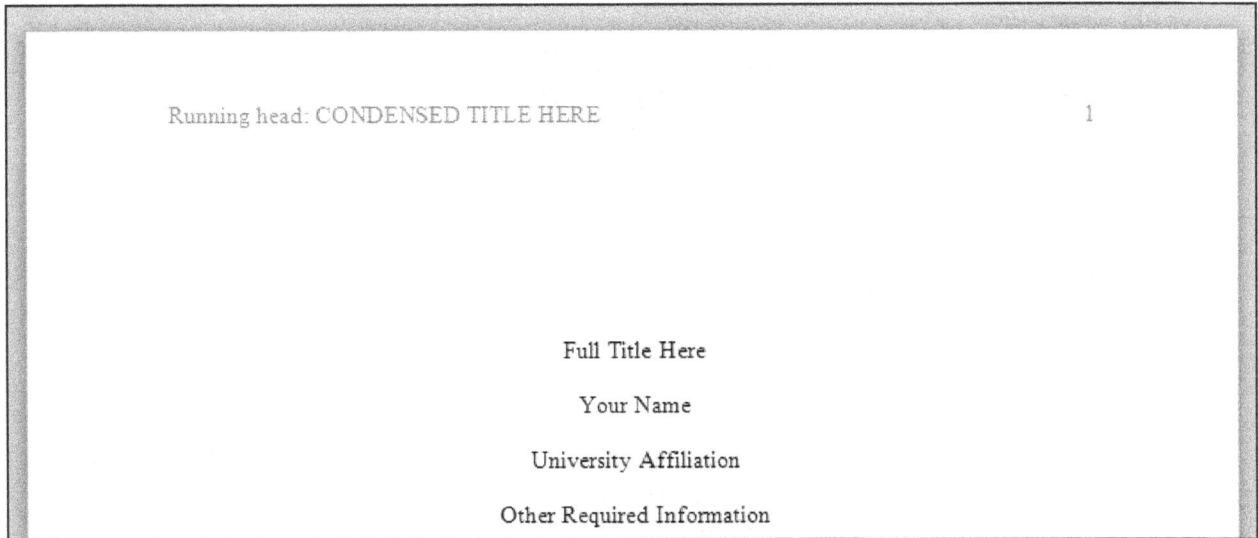

Running head: CONDENSED TITLE HERE   1

Full Title Here

Your Name

University Affiliation

Other Required Information

Figure 59. The cover page of the template

Here is the abstract page (page 2). See Figure 60.

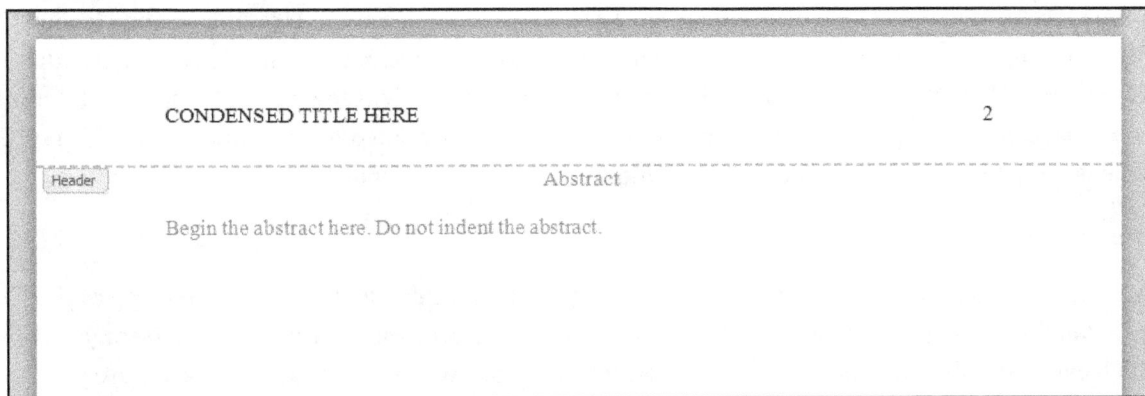

CONDENSED TITLE HERE   2

Header

Abstract

Begin the abstract here. Do not indent the abstract.

Figure 60. The abstract page of the template

Here is page 3, the introduction page. Note the title is repeated from the cover page and is not in boldface type. Indent all paragraphs one-half inch, as discussed previously (Figure 61).

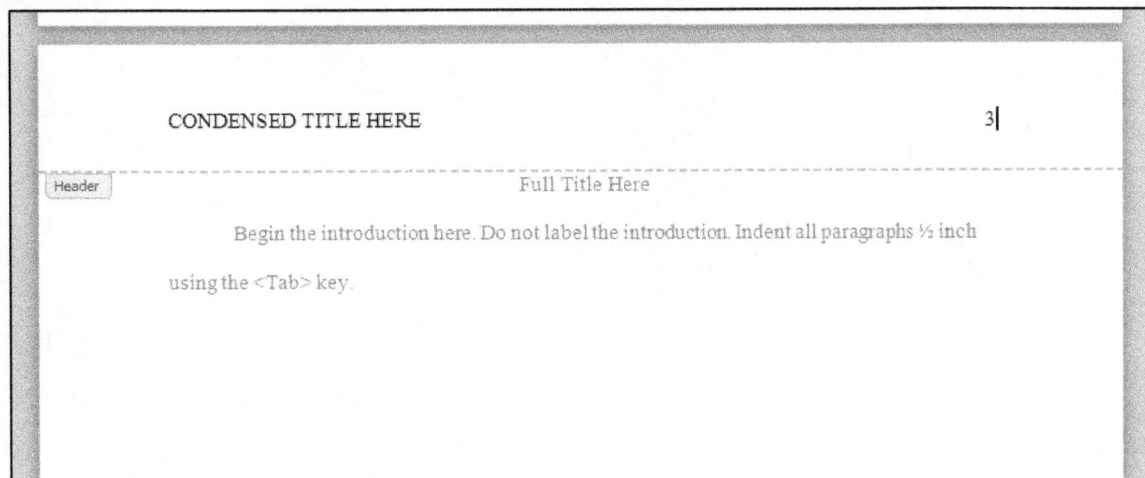

CONDENSED TITLE HERE   3

Header

Full Title Here

Begin the introduction here. Do not label the introduction. Indent all paragraphs ½ inch using the <Tab> key.

Figure 61. The introduction page of the template

When you are ready to begin the reference list, start a new page (Figure 62).

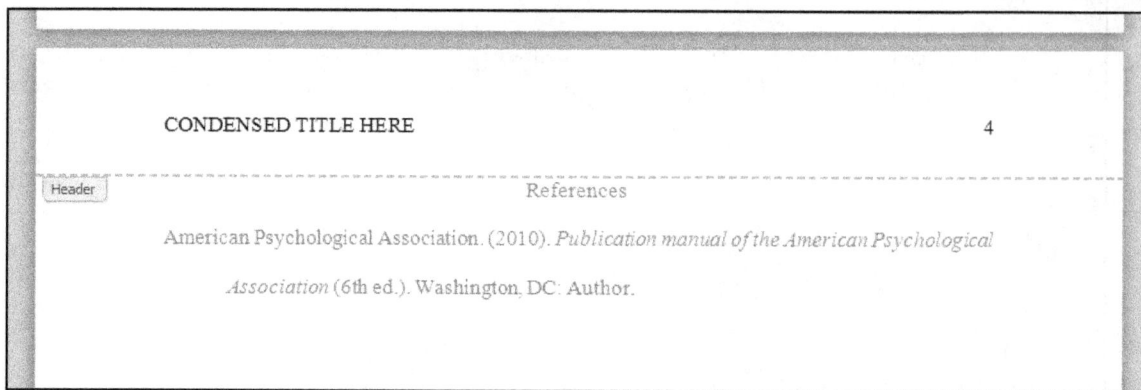

CONDENSED TITLE HERE   4

Header

References

American Psychological Association. (2010). *Publication manual of the American Psychological*

Association (6th ed.). Washington, DC: Author.

Figure 62. The reference page of the template

Using Your Template

To use your new template, locate it and open it. Save the new file as a Word document with an appropriate name to preserve the template for future use. All the formatting you applied to the template will be automatically applied to the document, and clicking on the Title, Normal, References, Heading 1, and Heading 2 icons in the Styles group will apply the correct font, formatting, margins, spacing, and indentation. Just edit the page headers to replace "CONDENSED TITLE HERE" with your actual condensed title in all caps. Edit the full title on the cover page and the top of page 3. Then simply remove the unwanted generic information and type your paper. This is a time saver because you have to build the template only once, and you can reuse it.

Another Way to Access a Template

Another way to access a template and apply it to your current document involves the use of the Developer tab. This tab does not appear by default, so you will have to select **File** > **Options** > **Customize Ribbon**. Now, locate the Developer tab in the left window and add it to the right window. Click OK (see Figure 63).

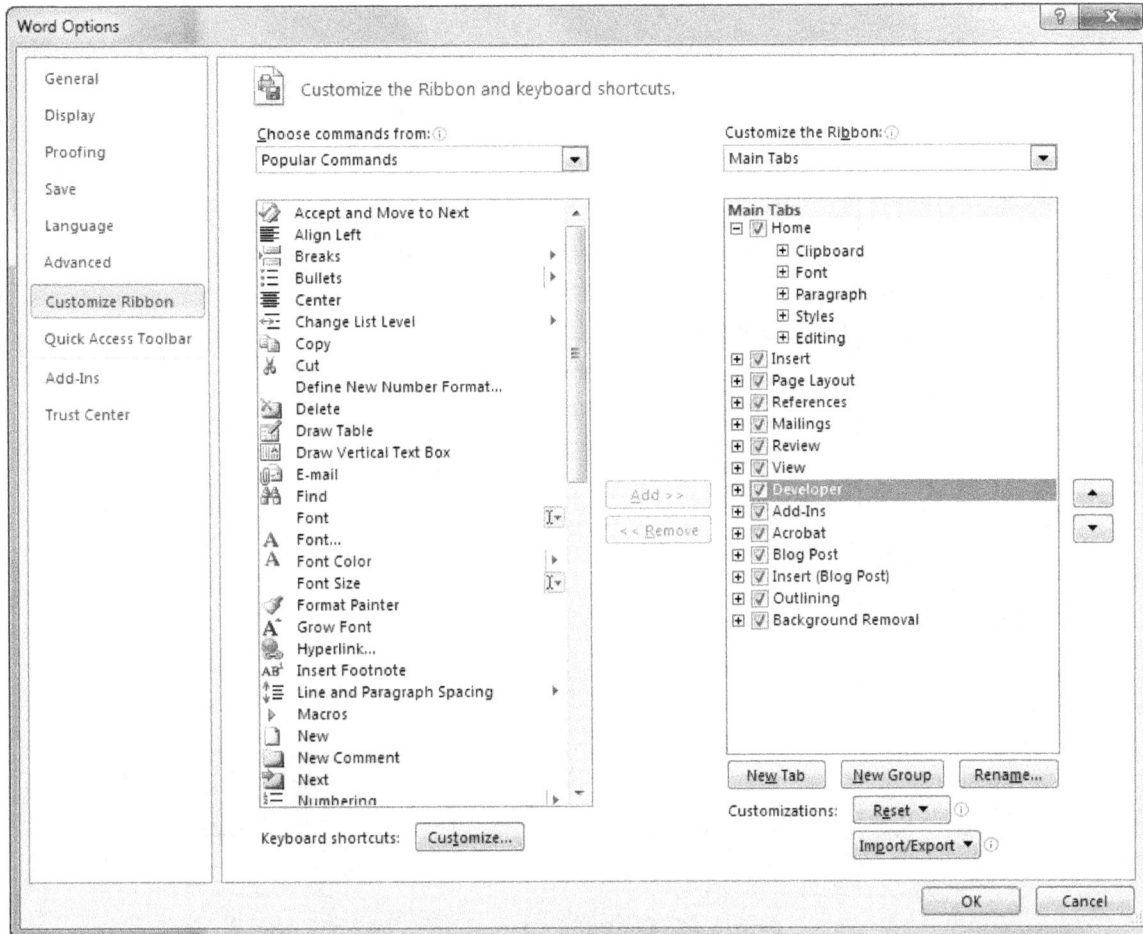

Figure 63. Adding the Developer tab to the ribbon

Now, you will have a Developer tab on your ribbon (Figure 64).

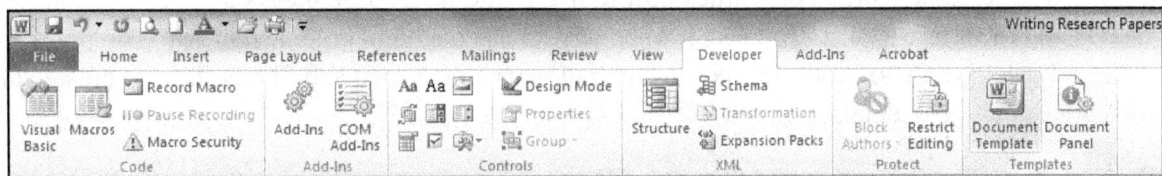

Figure 64. Accessing the Templates group

From this tab, select **Templates** > **Document Template**. You can now navigate to any template you have saved on your hard disk or other accessible medium. To apply the styles and other settings from the template you have added, just check Automatically update document styles (Figure 65).

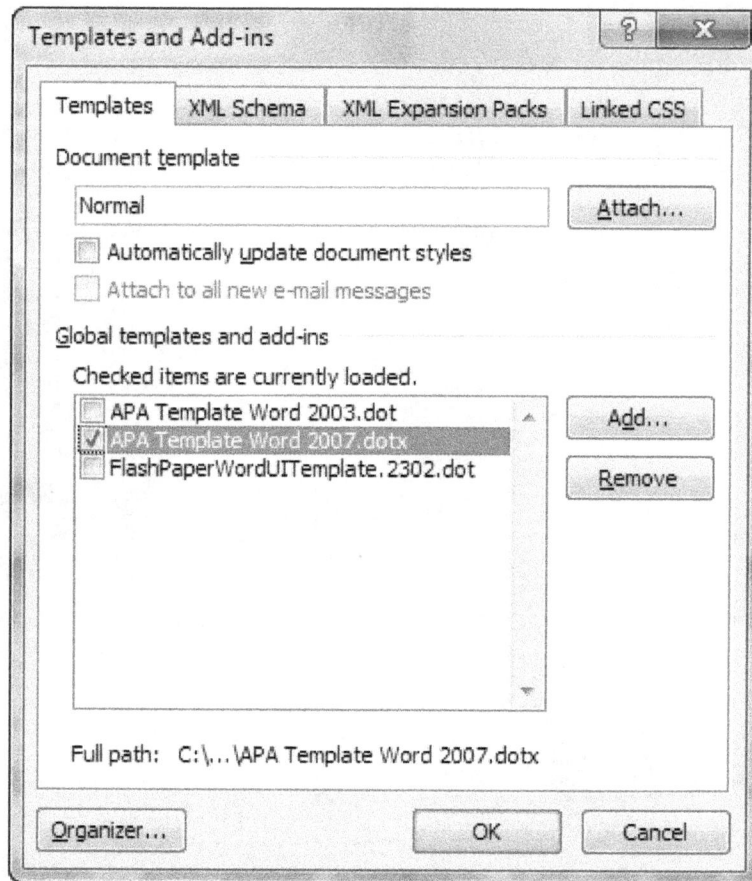

Figure 65. Applying a template to an open document

Conclusion and Final Thoughts

In this brief book, you have learned some of the finer points of writing research papers in APA style using the features of Microsoft Word. You learned how to use styles, insert page breaks and headers, and cite references in the text and the reference list. You also learned how to use the bibliographic tools of Word, how to format statistical results, how to avoid and fix some common writing errors, and finally, how to create your own reusable APA style document template.

The more you use these automated features of Word, the more you will enjoy them, and the more time you will save yourself. Any task you do more than once with your documents should be automated if possible. Your document template automates the styles, the line spacing, the margins, the page headers and page numbering, and the required indentation for the reference list.

Now that you have explored some of the useful features of Word, you may want to find out more about how to program Word to your advantage. It is fairly easy to make Word work together very well with the other programs in Microsoft Office. Just for some thought starters, I have used an Excel spreadsheet to store names and addresses, and then used Word's mail merge feature to send form letters or e-mails. I have also written macros in Word that automate certain repetitive text I type into student papers, such as generic comments. I have made Word tables that do math to summarize student grades using a grading rubric. Most students and faculty members are simply unfamiliar with these additional capabilities of Word, and even after you have mastered everything we discussed in this book, you will still have just scratched the surface of this very powerful program!

I love hearing from my readers, especially fellow teachers and students, so if you have anything (good or bad) to say about this book, especially if you find an error or have a suggestion for the inevitable second edition, please e-mail me at larry@twopaces.com.

References

Aaron, J. E. (2011). *Little, Brown compact handbook* (8th ed.). Boston, MA: Longman.

American Psychological Association. (2001). *Publication manual of the American Psychological Association* (5th ed.). Washington, DC: Author.

American Psychological Association. (2010). *Publication manual of the American Psychological Association* (6th ed.). Washington, DC: Author.

Durtschi, C., Hillison, W., & Pacini, C. (2004). The effective use of Benford's law to assist in detecting fraud in accounting data. *Journal of Forensic Accounting, 5,* 17-34.

Pace, L. A. (2012, January). *How they cheat: A statistical analysis of plagiarism and lazy writing.* Poster session presented at the meeting of the National Institute on the Teaching of Psychology, St. Pete Beach, FL.

Raimes, A, (2004). *Universal keys for writers.* New York, NY: Houghton Mifflin.

Rosnow, R. L., Rosenthal, R., & Rubin, D. B. (2000). Contrasts and correlations in effect-size estimation. *Psychological Science, 11*(6), 446-453.

Rosnow, R. L., & Rosnow, M. (1986). *Writing papers in psychology: A student guide.* Belmont, CA: Wadsworth.

Wilson, K. G. (1993). *The Columbia guide to standard American English.* New York, NY: Columbia University Press.

Warriner, J. E. (1988). *English composition and grammar* (4th course). Orlando, FL: Harcourt Brace Jovanvich.

Strunk, W. (1918). *Elements of style.* Retrieved from http://www.bartleby.com/141/strunk5.html#11

www.ingramcontent.com/pod-product-compliance
Lightning Source LLC
Chambersburg PA
CBHW051229200326
41519CB00025B/7312